FOR THOSE ABOUT TO CHANGE

Alfonso Vonscheidt
The Inspiralist

Inspiration for Creative Dreamers

The Hampstead House Publications

For Those About To Change

The Hampstead House Publications
London, May 2012

On-line Guides and Publications
www.thehampsteadhouse.wordpress.com

Introduction

Between you and me, this world is a mess, and most people haven't got a clue about what's going on, or where they are standing, in such a chaos.

But, whether you are a teenager looking wide-eyed at the overwhelming world around you, or a 'young-at-heart' who can't find its way in an overbearing society, you have a chance to 'unlearn' what you've been taught so far, and introduce your changes to the script, so the play unfolds in the sense you choose.

These times demand us to make sense of our place in the universe, the inner and the outer one. We can't pretend anymore 'we don't know', 'we don't understand', or 'we were not there'. We are here and now; we are building our future as we speak (or keep silent); we have duties and responsibilities: growing up, having fun, and making a difference for ourselves and for those around us.

The aim of this book is to inspire people to break with their routine existence, with confidence and a sense of purpose; transform themselves in order to achieve their goals, and, in the process, make a difference in the world.

You've got the loop

Rather than countless teachings and disciplines, there are just a few basic tenets which run forwards and backwards in space and time. They've been called archetypes, revelations, symbols, philosophy, bollocks, magic. They arose in ancient times as intuitive mysticism, later sustained by scientific methods, which also found that knowledge inspiring to keep digging into original concepts and feelings.

I see the treasure of human wisdom as a loop, feeding and being fed by the past and the future, with humans here and now imagining a fleeting present, a flash of time and space that lasts an instant, and then it's gone.

Nothing we know is real; everything is illusory, and the material world is highly dependent on our filtered perceptual capacity. Our values and possessions are permanently swept away by the winds of time as a moving twister, towards an imaginary future. The thing that holds the setup together is the group of basic tenets, with which we can play and shape the kind of reality we choose for ourselves at a particular moment, before it vanishes. The shadow of the wind, yesterday's clouds, a flash in the pan, reflect what we call reality.

That's also freedom, though; and that, nobody and nothing can take away from us.

Enough of theory and rhetoric! Let's get cracking.

What to do now?

Well, it's not the first time humankind is at a crossroads, and many people have already analysed the critical situation on their own time, explored options, taken stock of resources, designed plans and strategies, and decided to move forwards. Some people can afford to get stuck in a rut; others can't, and have to find alternative ways to take a leap ahead without safety net, only with the smallest hint of guts, hope and faith in themselves.

For those about to jump, we salute you!

The Threads of the Tapestry

One can choose between the 'go-get-it' approach and the 'go-with-the- flow' one. There is also the belief in a higher almighty power to solve our problems, and psycho-cybernetics which consider man as a guided missile with a target.

I say, there are different circumstances in an individual's life, different places, seasons and relationships. For these changing phases or stages, adequate techniques to cope, survive or grow can and must be applied. You can't kill a fly with a cannonball; you can't win with your hands tied. Sometimes quantity and power will trump quality and wisdom, and viceversa. Sometimes faith *will* move mountains, and other times, surfing the wave of neurolinguistic programming *will* set you free from a long lasting anguish. Randomly playing with magic pebbles, or exhaustively planning your financial future, might also work wonderfully, if you are into those rituals.

I personally believe that the human experience is too wide and deep to be tackled with a single stroke of genius, and that every bit of knowledge and technology conform a whole tapestry for us to contemplate and make choices upon it, for our benefit, using our innate capacity: the basic tenets.

Now, what exactly are those building blocks of wellbeing and development?

The Original Tenets

There are no careers or Universities that teach you with certainty how to live, to love, or to prosper, because for some reason, scholars and specialists haven't been open-minded enough to accept that we have a body, a mind and a soul; we are not unidimensional, each of the three play a part in our lives, and the state of maximum wellbeing we can aspire to, depends on an optimal harmony among those parts. Like a tripod bases its strength and stability on the respect and balance of its three legs, not of just one or two, what defines us as humans is a system with physical, creative and purposeful dimensions.

For ages, success based on integration and freedom from conflict and supremacy has been achieved by people who made a difference in their piece of the world. Tapping from Theology, Psychology or Philosophy, even when those labels hadn't been assigned yet to those disciplines, from Tradition and Common Sense, they found inspiration and motivation, confidence and hope, purpose and fulfilment. Many other characteristics emanated, and still emanate, as a by-product of the original tenets: diversity, progress, compassion.

You wouldn't turn away from the success of Apple, Google or Facebook, as symbols of the immediacy and globalization of our times. The world seems faster and smaller because of the impact of these technologies and social networks. Why, then, turning away from other figures such as Jesus, Buddha, Confucius, as timeless characters of spirituality, who symbolise the success you can get, when you follow the basic tenets to find essential fulfilment and wholeness? These images of internal wisdom and perfection have singlehandedly revolutionised the way of thinking and habits of millions, until these days. Leaders, armies and sportspeople thrive following their message. Why resisting personal development? Why not learning from the best? Why try and reinventing the wheel time and again?

It is about purpose, it is about meaning, and, worry not, also about health and wealth, satisfaction and happiness. What comes in between are by-products, not part of the basic, timeless and immutable building blocks. Aim at the ultimate goal, at the top of the ladder, not at a mere rung, and you'll be stepping confidently and effortlessly into the ultimate satisfaction, the realisation of your highest dreams.

FOR THOSE ABOUT TO CHANGE

The Banquet is Served – Help Yourself

Your life to date is the result of your past beliefs. Your future will be the result of the beliefs you choose to hold today. You are shaping your future, right now. It will be your choice to live a life of conventional limitation and minuscule potential, or a life of unlimited opportunities and infinite possibilities.

Decide today that you're going to upgrade your self-image to the very highest level, because this is the choice you have. You have the ability and the choice, right now, to exceed all your previous levels of accomplishment.

The way you think about yourself determines everything you say, do, believe and feel. The world around you is a reflection of your inner world. Whatever you see outside has a parallel inside you.

It's time then to redefine yourself according to the way you want to see it and to be seen by others. You are about to become someone who is self-made and to reject any outdated or damaging beliefs that were dumped on you by others. You will be the person you choose to be, a person you like and admire and love being. This doesn't mean you're going to be someone entirely different, because there are lots of qualities you'll want to keep. It just means you're shedding the stuff you no longer need, and creating a stronger, healthier more successful you, who has an easier, more enjoyable life.

To find you true ideal life you have to look a little further. What we actually want is far more than just money and possessions. The dream each person has is totally in keeping with who they are and, as a result, totally achievable. Think about what it is that really satisfies you – what gives you a sense of achievement. What absorbs you so much that you don't notice time passing. What it is that excites you, that you love doing so much you'd feel truly lucky to be able to do it all the time.

Most of us know, deep down, what we really want to be doing. But we normally keep it very private, because we think it's impossible to actually make a living doing something we enjoy so much. Perhaps it's a hobby at the moment; perhaps it's only a dream, but it's certainly there, somewhere.

If you want a happy, successful, abundant life then you must see yourself as happy, successful, talented and lucky person. Your self-image is your blueprint for success and will determine every aspect of your life, from the way you feel about yourself to the quality of your relationships and the job you are doing. The goals you are pursuing, the dreams you have, are far less likely to be achieved if your self-image is poor. Once you have a strong, healthy self-image in place then everything else will become easier and more straightforward.

Your subconscious mind has been successfully programmed by simple, repeated instructions and messages from others around you. As a result, certain beliefs have been created. In order to replace these old beliefs with new ones, you must do the same thing; in other words, reprogramme. This time you will choose the instructions and messages, and you will give them to your subconscious mind. The way to do this is through simple, repeated statements, affirmations. Repeated frequently, they create powerful new messages for your subconscious to absorb. Give yourself these messages as often as you can, dozens or even hundreds times a day – because that's how often you have the opposite, negative thoughts. Write your affirmations out and pin them up where you can see them; say them out loud when you can; look in the mirror and say them to yourself. You are what you think about all day long.

Who you say you are is confirmed by the way you speak about yourself. So it's vital that you give up self-deprecating, belittling and apologetic ways of talking about yourself right now. The way you speak will define you and if you talk this way people will instantly know that you have a low opinion of yourself.

Visualising means seeing in your mind's eye, the scene you want to create. Before you go to sleep, and again in the morning, picture your coming day's events and see yourself moving effortlessly and successfully during the day. See people responding in exactly the way you would wish.

A simple and brilliant way to enhance your new self-image is to act the part of the person you want to be.

High levels of self-worth and self-confidence are vital to a happy, successful life. They are the blocks with which you will build a hard core of self-belief. They separate exceptional human beings from the average and charismatic leaders from followers. Mastering these abilities brings serenity, security, self-acceptance and a profound sense of comfort and ease within yourself.

Everything you attract into your life is a reflection of what you feel you desire, what you feel you are worth and how highly you value yourself in all areas of life. The opportunities, the people, the breaks and the luck you attract are all a direct result of the messages you are sending out. The circumstances of your life – personal, professional and social – tell you everything about how you rate yourself.

Self-worth is the degree to which you like yourself, is a sense of internal composure that gives you complete freedom. Very few people enjoy a high level of personal comfort and ease. In most cases the slightest probing reveals that most people don't like themselves very much at all.

Western culture, religious teaching and, in many cases, parental conditioning all taught us as children that to think well of ourselves and feel good about ourselves is vain, selfish, and wrong. The attitude was, and often still is, that if children are encouraged to think of themselves as special they will grow up to be intolerable adults, vain, selfish and arrogant, seeing themselves as superior and everyone else as less worthy. The truth is, only when we have been fed huge amounts of appreciation, love and generosity as children and taught to like ourselves, we can be free to extend the same appreciation, love and generosity to others. People who are brought up to like and feel good about themselves become happier, more successful, kinder and nicer people.

The Feelgood Factor

The feelgood factor is a state of being in which you genuinely like and are profoundly at ease with yourself, and you generate immense enthusiasm and optimism for life. Most of us look for this feelgood factor outside ourselves, through compliments, a pay rise, a new car or a trophy girlfriend, which only bring temporary satisfaction. Without this feelgood factor you will go through life without the support of the most constant, ever-present potential ally you will ever have… yourself. All of us come into the world on our own and we leave on our own. At some point in between, it makes sense to get comfortable with ourselves. So, making peace with yourself, getting comfortable in your own skin on your own terms, befriending yourself and backing yourself 100 percent throughout life, is the ultimate and only route to internal security and external optimism.

The feelgood factor is like a safety net that allows you to follow your desires, take risks and lead the sort of life you want to live as opposed to the life that you or anyone else think you should live. Without this safety net, you will always be looking for security and status, approval and respect.

Your feelgood factor has nothing to do with arrogance or isolation. It is unhappy people with low self-worth who tend to be the most self-focused and who can be socially withdrawn, brooding and even antagonistic. Happy people, by contrast, are generally found to be more sociable, flexible and creative, and are more able to tolerate life's frustrations. They are also more loving and forgiving, towards themselves and others.

To Question or not to Question

There is a feeling of affinity and goodwill towards others that can only occur when we have taken care of ourselves, and taken responsibility for generating our own happiness. Generosity and 'bigness' of character can only flourish when we have provided for ourselves and have plenty over to share.

Think hard about your religious and spiritual beliefs and practices. A religion that condemns you as being an unworthy sinner and requires you to spend the rest of your life atoning for your sins, is not the ideal backdrop for feeling good about yourself as a human being. The ideas that underpin many religions are very pervasive in our culture, and tend to seep under your skin. Question the parts of your religion that require you to see yourself as being intrinsically bad. Many people are finding that organised religion no longer meets their needs, and are no longer providing satisfying answers to our spiritual and moral questions; we are experiencing the urge to come up with our own intensely personal answers, as part of the movement to take back responsibility for the core values that we hold. We are gifted human beings with this wonderful human intelligence, and all human beings have the capacity to be very determined and to direct that strong sense of determination in whatever direction they would like to use it. With this approach you can get up off your knees and give up atoning, concentrating instead on bringing forth positive qualities such as tolerance, respect and kindness to yourself and others. Surely you deserve the best, and you have a responsibility to honour yourself and take care of yourself in mind, body and spirit. Showing yourself disrespect, through habits such as overeating, drinking excess alcohol or smoking, makes no sense. Nor does allowing others to be disrespectful towards you. Honour, value and respect your natural gifts, against anybody else's views or interests.

Lovingkindness

Are you a big, generous, expansive human being? More and more people are taking the decision to give time, energy and effort to others. You don't have to give huge amounts of time to a charity. You can consciously carry out little acts of kindness on a daily basis that don't require much extra time, just extra thought. Look after the most vulnerable people you know: children and the elderly. You can inspire children with well-chosen words that could really make a difference. Listening with interest and concern to an elderly man or woman on a bus, may just make a difference to their day. And if you do decide to volunteer some of your time you'll feel terrific about yourself, you'll see your problems with less intensity and become more relaxed about your own issues.

Giving selflessly brings with it a unique feeling of having made a contribution in a way that paid work doesn't. Make a contribution, make a difference, and make your life important. Being good requires active service.

Sometimes, if someone is concerned about bringing more balance and fulfilment into their life, suggest them that deeper meaning and satisfaction may be found through giving time and effort to others.

Wipe the Slate Clean

Clean, shiny, pristine self-worth requires a clear conscience. Low-level guilt lives under your skin, pervades your whole being and eats away at your self-worth. Take this opportunity to detox, have a personal spring clean and rid yourself of any dust and grime. Clearing past misdeeds, wrongdoings and mistakes paves the way for greater clarity and optimism. You'll feel lighter, cleaner and ready to sparkle.

First check your interpretation of events. Second, make amends. If you have decided that you were really in the wrong then do something about it. Apologise, make a phone call, send a bunch of flowers or write a letter, and then let go of the guilt. Guilt is a sign that something needs putting right. Third, do something practical. If you've really caused damage then do something tangible to re-balance the scales. If you can't alter the original situation then make a contribution that is as relevant as possible.

Someone with a magnetic personality attracts into their lives favourable people and circumstances. You create a magnetic personality by building your foundations of self-image, self-worth and glowing self-confidence and having high-quality thoughts about yourself. You have attracted everything in your life. So, why not make sure that you attract only the best: the most loving, reliable, supportive people, the most favourable circumstances, the great pieces of luck and plenty of resources.

Appreciate yourself for all that you do and are, and be more generous to others, especially the more vulnerable among us.

Self-reliance

It is the most useful attribute that you can develop. With powerful and healthy levels of self-reliance, you will never again look to others to sort, fix, mend or organise your life for you. You will understand that you alone are responsible for the life you have, and that you alone are able to create it. Self-reliance is like a muscle, you can use it or lose it. People who are self-reliant stand out because they have learned to look inside themselves for answers and solutions. In doing so, they have developed a happy and healthy relationship with themselves.

Those who are completely self-reliant have real power. What is normally considered to be power is not real power at all. You can be rich, successful and neurotic. If you rely on money as the source of your power, you'll live on a knife edge, with the fear that it could all be taken away from you. Trying to win people over, seeking approval and acceptance, trying to impress and craving praise all create weakness and destroy your real power, because they make you dependent on other people's whims. You end up being a puppet controlled by others' moods and choices.

Self-importance is very different to self-worth. Self-importance is what insecure people hide behind, in an attempt to convince others that they matter. Real power comes from self-reliance; it gives internal power to stand out from others, freedom to speak your mind, and live as you please. What could be better than to have the confidence not to care about whether people take you seriously or not, but instead to live with your own respect and approval?

The self-reliance masterplan

Being your own best friend is the most powerful thing you can do for yourself. Sometimes I hear people say the most insulting thing about themselves, without realising how much they are undermining and demoralising themselves.

Powerful people talk less. Powerful people don't waste words, waffle on about nothing in particular or drift from one piece of chat to another. They think about what they want to say and express those thoughts clearly and purposefully to the relevant people. They don't need to sell themselves to anyone because they are already sold to themselves. They never argue, for there is no point to be scored, no position to defend. Those who know do not speak, those who speak do not know.

The most powerful way to speak is with brevity, with nothing to prove and no need to impress, dominate the conversation or hear yourself talk. Make a point of listening at least twice as much as you talk, without thinking of your reply as the other person is talking. When you listen fully in this way the other person will feel supported in your presence. You can let go of any need to dominate, persuade or compete. You will feel deeply secure, simply through your ability to listen and be silent. Most people talk for talking's sake. They exaggerate, invent things, talk without knowing or understanding what they're talking about, or go over and over the same thing. They waste huge amounts of energy defending their point of view, and trying to persuade others to share it. Don't bother trying to impress people; don't talk unless you have something to say, and then keep it simple.

For Those About To Change

The past has relevance to your future. Because you are the historian to your own past, you have the power to change a negative memory into a positive memory. What was once a bad memory will be balanced with some good memories. Review memories with a positive focus. Questions play a major role in your mental well-being. You use them to get information about yourself, life, experiences, the past and the future.

Living the life you truly desire does not involve a problem-free existence. There are situations in life that may be beyond your control, but the mind has a benevolent predisposition that both invites and allows control.

Police your Subconscious Mind

Your brain attempts to find an answer to every question posed. A negative question often leads to a negative answer. Such is the power of the subconcious mind, that if you firmly plant a message on it, it can become more real than any subsequently intellectual reasoning. Your conscious mind presents information that the subconscious assumes is real, but the subconscious mind does not distinguish between what is real and what is not.

That's why you need to monitor your thought process, and be careful about the information you could inadvertently feed in. You may know on one level that you are perfectly capable of doing something, and yet somewhere along the line you question your ability so badly, that many times you draw a mental blank over the simplest tasks.

Solve the Problem!

The way in which you define a problem will affect how you deal with it. Your whole being, physical and mental, is at a standstill when you are blocked.

Some people find it hard to accept that life doesn't always go according to plan. Just as you have your own particular agenda, so does everyone else. Just as you are prone to changing your mind, so are others. What was once a shared goal may no longer remain one. Accepting that problems go with the territory stops you asking the 'Why me?' questions. Life is not out to get you; it's just a case of recognising that mutual synchronicity causes few interruptions to your running order, while a lack of synchronicity causes a lot. The real solution is to take responsibility for your problems and not resort to blaming other people.

Deal with the cause, not the symptom. Bring the situation back to yourself and take possession of the problem. Be clear about how it affects you and the part you play in the situation. If you think you play no part, then you are excluding yourself from finding a solution. There are bound to be times when people interfere in your life. The options are: put up with it, moan about it, play the victim and be at the mercy of others. Or deal with it by finding a solution to the problem.

The format that allows you to deal with problems involve you allocating a time to think about a problem, find a solution and put the plan into action. It is surprising how little time is specifically allocated to dealing with problems. They get jumbled up with other thoughts that also need space and refuse to go away. Instead, they pop up in your mind when you least expect them, and when they are least welcome.

The Mental Oasis

Spend a few minutes recalling an event that gives you the feel-good factor. It could be a good film, your favourite meal, intimate time with a loved one, a beautiful day. You are looking for a memory that puts you in a relaxed frame of mind and one that is easy to conjure up in your head. Write the event down in your journal, creating as detailed a picture as possible. It helps to bring the senses into play, so recall smell, taste, sound, colours and sensations. You will use this memory as your mental oasis: a place to enter, leave and re-enter. It's worth setting some time aside – say ten minutes a day for the next few days – to focus on your mental oasis, to get in the habit of quickly turning into it. You can prepare your surroundings, i.e. find a quiet area where you won't be interrupted, play some relaxing music, remove any tight-fitting clothing, sit in a comfortable chair, spend a few minutes concentrating on your breathing.

Excuses are little voices in our heads telling us why we can't do something. When people say: 'The reason I'm not doing so and so' they mean 'the excuse for not doing so and so'. The 'why' question becomes useful the minute you start to ask 'Why not?' Presented with a challenge, you can either slip into a mind-set that looks for umpteen reasons as to why it is not achievable, or one that looks for ways to overcome the challenge. The distinguishing factor is attitude. Which one will you choose?

People who achieve goals stand out through attitude, through their determination to succeed even against odds. That involves not only seizing opportunities, but also creating them: otherwise, you could spend a lifetime regretting 'what might have been', and thinking 'if only', more times than you would like. An obvious cause of excuses is fear. If you keep giving yourself reasons for not doing something, the chances are you won't do it.

Write out one of your goals in the top of a page. On the right-hand side list as many reasons as you can for achieving that goal. On the left-hand side of the page list all the reasons you can think of for not achieving your goal. You'll find that all your apparent weaknesses can be converted into opportunities.

Setting out goals takes you into new territory. It can feel like opening the door on something new; it's all too easy to feel tempted to run back to the security of familiar ground.

Sabotaging your own goals is an all too common phenomenon. Going back to the previous exercise, work on eliminating any answers involving other people. Unless you constantly bring the goal back to yourself, the responsibility of achieving lies with someone else. Making it somebody else's fault lets you off the hook.

To go for the easy option all the time is a fast way to lose sight of your goal. If you are good at finding excuses, try putting some of that creative ability into finding solutions. The results are much more rewarding.

A person's thinking processes are governed by how they anticipate events. The tendency we have when we don't know the answer is to fill the gap with what we think must be the answer. Fear persuades people to predict the worst possible outcome. In order to succeed you have to remain positive. This becomes difficult when your point of reference is blurry, or clouded by negative memories. Information is the key to creating a positive association. The brain has access to past and present information to anticipate a future event, but it also likes to predict future information.

Example: you may have a goal to run your own business. Existing memories tell you that you have no experience in the field of accountancy and cannot afford to bring in a bookkeeper. This could be seen as a good excuse not to pursue that goal. On the other hand, you may sign up for a bookkeeping course, and thereby eliminate a prediction for future failure.

Every time you make an excuse for not pursuing a particular goal, you are filling in the missing blanks with negative anticipation. Whether you have gone down that road before, or are visiting it for the first time, the association has to be positive. This is where you can further your development skills, so for example, if your goal is to get a new job, you would want to gather as much information as possible about the vacancy before the interview. You may be required to brush up on existing skills, or learn a few new skills in order to be the most sensible candidate. The more information you have the better, as this can steer you away from repeating past experiences and prevent you from falling foul of undesirable future ones.

Read your goals daily to keep your brain on alert mode. When the goal is at the forefront of your mind, useful information or opportunities are less likely to escape your attention. Review the contribution you have made to your file of useful information on a weekly basis. The more information you gather, the more real the goal becomes. By contributing daily, the goal feels like an integral part of your life, not some distant daydream. Remember that when fear and uncertainty creep in, the missing blanks in your game plan are usually filled with false and negative answers.

Never underestimate the power of positive visualisation. At any given time, your brain is predicting the outcome of events. Actions are governed by thought processes. If failure is what you predict, you should find no problem setting the wheels in motion to achieve just that.

There is no guarantee that success is waiting for you around the corner. The most successful people experience setbacks, but that's exactly how they see them – as setbacks, not failures. Being positive definitely affects your recovery rate. Do you really know anyone who has never experienced disappointment? It's something we all go through. The difference is that the positive person swallows the bitter pill, whereas the negative person scoffs the whole bottle. Obviously it takes far longer to recover from an overdose, than just a mouthful of unpleasant medicine.

If you use up all the megabytes in your mental computer it's time to offload. There are only so many thoughts that can be held at one time. When you get stuck in a negative mind-set, the positive thoughts struggle to find a way in.

It's crucial not to overlook the importance of recognising the symptoms that occur when the body is put under strain. Similar symptoms are experienced when the mind is put under strain. Look at panic attacks. Any victim will tell you that they felt like they were dying:

their heart was racing, bursting out of their chest, shaking was common, sweating, breathlessness, an overwhelming feeling of fear.

We are emotional beings and subject to a whole range of feelings. What the brain refuses to acknowledge the body will take on board. The mind can play a big part in getting us over-excited. Calming the thought processes can alleviate the onset of new symptoms and reduce the effect of existing ones. There are also ways to administer a bit of tender loving care when the body cries out for it. Parents comfort a crying child with soothing words and actions. They create both a mental and physical oasis. Combining the two produces the best results. Recalling your mental oasis, the advantage of this technique is that you have allocated time to deal with a problem. Unless an urgent decision is required, the brain quickly accepts the new routine of thinking and dealing with problems at the appropriate time. This gives you mental breathing space. The important factor is to recognise the reactions and signals given off by your body, and treat them.

Time management and Making the right decision

If you want to make changes in your life, you have to create the space to do it. Much of this process is to do with how you manage your own time. Time affects the decisions you make, so it's important to look at how you prioritise your time, or set aside time to make decisions. You also need to find out whether you are caught up in the past, or are able to embrace the future, allowing time for goals and providing the time to bring into your life what you truly desire.

It is easy to gather things, and how hard it is to let them go. But letting go can be very liberating. Possessions can remain an extension of your personality without being a useless accessory. When you decide to bring new things into your life, there is no need to hold on to many of the old things.

Creating space

If something holds a strong sentimental value ask yourself the following questions. Is the memory a good one or bad one? Is it keeping my attention in the past and stopping me moving forward? How would it affect me if I no longer had this possession?

Imagine you could only keep a box full of items from each room you've cleared. You'll soon see how it affects your selection process. Once you have placed any items of real value in a box it's a lot easier to deal with what's left. If you didn't wear something last season, are you likely to wear it next season?

Fear of painful memories can keep you blocked from embracing change, and wanting to freeze a moment in time can also keep you blocked.

You can't see what's in front of you if you are always looking back. Allowing yourself to let go is the best test. Look around your home: are you building a shrine or a sanctuary?

As human beings, our survival instincts supply the basics: food, warm and shelter. Progressing beyond these, you invest time in creating your shelter. Comfort is often a high priority. You mark out your territory in a manner that reflects both your needs and mood. But sometimes that happens on a subconscious level. Your environment may start off cheerful and yet something happens along the way. You can stop it both mentally and physically. A physical clear-out is a great way for you to proceed to a mental clear-out.

Waking up everyday to familiar surroundings can cause you to become visually immune. That's not to say you aren't feeling the effects on many other levels.

Keeping the Mind Healthy

Under normal circumstances the brain has an enormous facility to store memory. To develop this, it's important to keep feeding the brain new information, by learning new skills, stretching your mental capacities with brain-teasers and playing word games, as well as doing crosswords and other memory-enhancing exercises.

Healthy minds have a better ability to concentrate and focus when you are dealing with the situations that life throws at you. It helps when you can keep your attention on one thing at a time. Time management doesn't just involve what you do with your time, it also has a lot to do with what you do with your mind during that time.

The Time Management Challenge

Successful people and achievers don't have more hours in the day than you do. The lady who is always late for appointments doesn't have fewer. There are certainly many practical applications that you can use to produce immediate results, but only if you are prepared to take responsibility for administering them. Your own time is relative to you. Others make demands on it, at times impose on it and even invade it, but ultimately only you can truly delegate it.

Separate your short-term goals from your long-term ones. To keep things simple, keep short-term goals as goals you wish to achieve within a three-month period, and view your long-term goals as any you will achieve thereafter. Write a date for achieving that goal. Write down your commitments in your diary/calendar: your mental preparation is underway. All you have to do now is make the time to follow through with the practical application.

Trying to fit goals into an already overloaded schedule will not produce the results you desire. At one end of the scale there is the lack of fulfilment and apathy that sets in from not pursuing the life you desire, and at the other end of the scale there is a fatigued, overworked and overwhelmed individual. Both situations cause stress. In some cases you'll need to offload some of the demands being made of you, rather than use time management to create more space in an already over-loaded day.

Once you know what you are doing with your time, you can decide what you actually want to do with it. The issue of time seems to cause the greatest dilemma with people who refuse to accept any responsibility for how they delegate it, preferring to claim that other people control their time.

List all the reasons why you have little or no control over your time. What you need to find out is if you are the major culprit. Apply the 'no more excuses'. By eliminating excuses you can get to the source of the block.

Time is valuable, indeed precious. You can try compensating, but you can't recapture a time gone by. To help you prioritise your time, look at your values. Remind yourself of what's important to you. This will help you to make the right choice. But this is not easy. Have your values paramount in your mind before you make a decision that will influence the demands made of your time and the consequences it will have on your life.

Procrastination

Just as decisions influence your time, time will also influence your decisions.

If taking a particular job seems like the right decision at the time, you have to make sure that you are weighing up all the pros and cons. Your work situation can influence other areas of your life. You may not be giving enough thought to the demands made on your time, how the job affects family life, the levels of stress that are incurred, the overall job satisfaction and how you will maintain a balance with the other vitally important areas of your life. Work takes up a major part of most people's day. If there are more minuses than pluses, a large part of your day is being spent somewhere you don't want to be.

How many people hold on to relationships well after their sell-by date, continue to maintain the company of people they don't particularly like, and constantly battle to overcome procrastination.

Procrastination seems to take a strong hold when the major part of your days feel compromised. You are stuck doing things you don't want to do. Be aware of the decisions you make which have consequences, and which will influence the running order of your day.

Are you fit for life?

Change will push you beyond your normal boundaries; you need to see beyond the limiting patterns that may be keeping you blocked.

Mental stamina is phenomenally powerful. It's no wonder that your body struggles to keep up with it. Although your body is equally capable of high performance, the problem arises when the two of you are out of sync. You may start off with a healthy body, but when your energy levels sink, apathy soon gets in. An active mind can lead to hours of studious learning, but without the necessary exercise and nutrients your body will experience atrophy. The two are dependent on each other. To maximise one you have to service the other.

When you consider that the skin you are born with is the largest organ in the body and the only overcoat you get, it does seem strange to spend more on replaceable accessories. What you do with your disposable income is very much a case of personal preference. However, you have to be in a position to enjoy it.

Looking after your body puts you in the best position to go in prepared for the next challenge. There is no doubt that keeping the brain active will keep you mentally alert. Goals give you a sense of purpose, a reason to get out of bed in the morning. That's why you need to keep setting goals. Your mental and physical preparation is equally important.

The focus in losing weight, drinking less, stop eating chocolate, giving up junk food, means depriving yourself of something that you probably enjoy. In the case of the goal 'lose weight', you may be reinforcing a very negative body image.

If you group together the goals that involve giving something up – chocolate, junk food, alcohol – you are keeping the focus of your brain on those things. So if you constantly keep reminding yourself not to eat chocolate, there's a good chance you will trigger an almighty craving for it. After all, you'll be thinking about it more than usual. Then, when you do give in to the temptation, you'll feel bad about your lack of willpower. Each time you are doing battle with yourself and unwittingly setting yourself up for failure. Your willpower is winning the day because it wants the chocolate. You have planted a really strong message in both the conscious and subconscious mind and the message is – I want chocolate, now!

Having a goal to get in shape and improve fitness levels is far less likely to reinforce a negative body image. You might consider enrolling at a gym or fitness class, increasing development skills and congratulating yourself on your achievements.

It's just a case of incorporating changes that will move you forward. Often, breaking a problem down allows you to find a workable solution. Because thoughts govern your action, your goal has to be positive to allow you to think about it in a positive way and trigger the necessary motivation to achieve it. To keep your motivation flowing you have to remind yourself of the progress you are making, so use your file and journal. If you are struggling to list achievements and developments skills, review your goals again. Make sure they are not worded in such a way as to keep you blocked.

Sometimes we create such a block for ourselves that self-esteem takes a real battering in the process. You have to set goals that move you forward rather than using ones that merely identify the problem and keep you stuck. The best way to climb any mountain is to take a step at a time.

You can walk more, take the stairs instead of the lift, play some music and dance around the room, practice breathing techniques, and do some gentle stretches.

Make a list of all the things you can do to improve your health chart. Get up earlier and practise breathing techniques; buy a juicer and kick off the day with a high energy drink; walk to work; cut out the health section from magazines; drink more water; get some leaflets from the local health club. You should be aiming to contribute to your health on a daily basis. By exploring every avenue you will soon see how easy it is to begin with small changes and work up to bigger ones. By gradually making changes to your routine it's much easier to make them an integral part of your life. All good work-outs start with a warm-up.

When you make progress with any goal your motivational bank account is rewarded. When your self-esteem is low, a better approach is to find ways of overcoming the minor hurdles and work your way up to the bigger ones. If a previous goal has always seemed out of reach, you may be inadvertently repeating old patterns that result in failure. Start off with some minor changes and watch your confidence grow.

Remember to set goals that will put you in a positive frame of mind. Have affirmations to reinforce your personal strengths and achievements. Look at your problems as challenges to be worked through and overcome and remember to make out an action plan for dealing with these. Continually gather information for your folder to inspire you with ideas and new skills to develop and add to your achievement list every time you make progress in this area.

Brain on Alert Mode

As with your other goals, information will help to move you forward. Information has a way of presenting itself when you request it. Sometimes a mental request is enough. The explanation for this is that you have put your brain on alert mode. Information that may have previously escaped your attention is no longer overlooked.

So many individuals have achieved a goal only to find it didn't have the desired result. It didn't make them feel how they thought it would. Without putting aside some time for self-exploration, it's very difficult to be in touch with what's really important to you. Some people learn this the hard way when they experience a loss, or put all their energies into pursuing goals that are not rewarding, or push themselves to the brink of a physical and mental breakdown.

With every goal you set (meditate, go to church, charity), take the time to question yourself if you are doing it for yourself or to impress/please others. Do you feel you have something to prove, and if so, what? Have you really explored the reasons behind why you want this goal? Does this goal reflect your value system and spiritual/religious path?

There is some point in achieving something for the sake of achievement alone. True success can only be defined on a personal level, which involves thinking about what would make you happy rather than what would gain attention or impress others. The achievement is usually the most enjoyable part of the whole process. Even when you really want to achieve a goal, you can feel a sense of anticlimax at the point when it is realised. Not because the goal is not a worthy one for you, but because you feel somewhat dependent without something to work for and put your energy into. It's fun working on your own projects, and as one nears completion, it's time to give some thought to the next one. Otherwise, you standstill. Without something to work on, you can't see what progress you have made, and you will quickly feel like you are slipping back rather than moving forward. You may see each goal as a very separate project, but that is a tricky plan to work with. However much you try to keep the areas of your life separate, you can't, because you are the one element common to every level. And into them you take your values, beliefs, code of conduct, opinions and every other component that makes you the individual you are.

Tell Me What You Really, Really Want

The important thing is to become familiar with identifying what it is you want. If someone is going to burst the bubble, you should be the one to do it. The biggest block you contend with is yourself. You can find lots of excuses and you can even hide behind your own belief system. Be aware of what is holding you back. If you feel that a particular belief system was engrained in you as a child, you can question what your own beliefs are and find a way to incorporate them into your life.

Change demands people to explore areas that they have been avoiding. People experience a huge gulf, but are unable to pinpoint where it is coming from. Write down what you want and why you want it. If something is getting in the way of your goals, write it down and work on how you will deal with it. If you can fin the problem the solution is waiting in line. Keep an open mind. The minute you think you have got a solution, be prepared to address the possibility that you've overlooked something.

Work

For most of us, the working day takes up a major part of our lives, so it's important to get the most from your job. When it comes to the work you do, how clear are you about why do you do it?

'Job insecurity' has become a mantra, as if it were something new that had never previously posed a threat. Technology has made some of the old skills redundant, and created gaps for new ones. It's prudent to arm yourself with information. Then you can see that change is the norm rather than stability.

The culture of a company can make a huge impact on your working life. So it's worth knowing if they are family-friendly, offer term-time contracts, childcare, job sharing, ongoing training, stress management. Whatever your civil status, you will have requirements for your well-being in the workplace, which go beyond financial security and job satisfaction. Technology has without a doubt upped the pace of the changes taking place; life is not stationary anywhere within a company, so it's no good closing your eyes and hoping for the best. The individuals who feel they have no control or choice, are the ones who experience the greatest stress.

The Stress Factors

How you view stress depends on how it affects you. You can reduce the effects of stress when you find ways to control what is going on around you. One of the things you can always control is your perception of what's going on. You can look at what upsets you, why you feel the way you do, and what you could do to feel differently.

Vegging out in front of the TV is not unnecessarily the best way to unwind after a stressful day. You'll benefit more from having interests outside work that allow you to switch off, such as regular exercise, eating a healthy diet, using breathing or relaxation techniques, talking your problems over with someone or uniting them down. They'll look a whole less threatening on paper and that can make it easier to find solutions. 20 percent of Britain's workforce is having personal problems, and 30 percent of the adult population suffer from aggression and anxiety at some stage of their working life.

If you are experiencing stress in the workplace, and there is little if anything on offer from your employers, make a commitment to yourself to do something about it. Some jobs are obviously more stressful than others by the very nature of the work involved, and the pressure that goes with those jobs is part of the daily routine. Working under pressure is not necessarily harmful: you may find it a positive thing and work better that way. The problems arise when you exceed the level of pressure you can cope with, and your mental and physical health suffer in the process. Most people find it very difficult to express dissatisfaction without it leading to conflict. And many people suffer in silence for fear of conflict. This can be a good time to practise your skills of communication. By writing out what you want to say in advance, there's less chance of getting side-tracked.

However skilled you are at your job, that is no indication that you have the ability to manage others. The essence of coaching is to look at yourself first. Trying to find someone else to blame slows down the whole process. You can't change your life is you keep passing the buck. If good staff training is not part of the culture of your workplace you have to find a way to deal with it. Leaving your present employment is not always a feasible option and if you remain unaware of the part you play, old problems can follow you into a new working environment.

All types of work involve interpersonal relationships and while some professions and more people-oriented than others, you will nearly always be dealing with people, be they clients or fellow workers. Every job has some form of pressure or stress to it and, with more companies downsizing, longer working hours for the most part are on the increase.

Finances

Money alone is never enough to compensate when other areas of your life are out of balance. When you're running a business, a lot of your value is tied up in that business, and if a dispute takes place the dynamics quickly change. Money often becomes the issue that controls the resulting power struggle. Leaving behind a high salary means you have to let go of something, which can be a way of life, possessions, or your home. You may not realize how important your finances are to you until they are put under threat. Panic quickly sets in and you'll find yourself desperately trying to hold on to what you've got.

A question you probably haven't explored is 'What would it take for me to feel secure'?

Would an annual medical check up make you feel secure about your health?

Would a strong belief and commitment make you feel secure in your faith?

Would a supportive boss make you feel secure in your work?

Would a loving partner make you feel secure in your relationship?

Would a supportive family make you feel secure?

Would a stimulating social life and loyal friends make you feel secure?

I'm sure most of you believe that money isn't everything. But just as money can allow you to enjoy the finer things in life, it can also stop you when it dictates every decision you make. Finances have to be kept in perspective. Knowing what's really important to you and what you truly value puts you in a position to make the right decisions and, if necessary, let go of something.

It's a question of letting go of the fear that controls many people's lives. Fear blocks your progress and prevents you from moving forward. Sometimes, when you let of the fears and tensions that have been taking you over, your financial situation doesn't get worse, it gets better. The reason is you have total control over it. When you appreciate that your life is worth more than your financial value, it will give you the courage to move forward.

The psychology of how people relate to money is baffling. Manufacturers know that is some goals are priced too cheaply, the consumer assumes they're low quality. Price them too high, and you could exclude your target market. Only you can truly know what you've comfortable with, and believe you deserve. Regardless of what level you are pitching at, there will always be those who question your value, so don't be disheartened and think it only happens to you. Just because some people question your value, it doesn't mean you are worth less.

When it comes to placing a financial value on yourself, you are worth exactly what you are prepared to accept. You have to know your bottom line. You have to be comfortable with the value you set for yourself, otherwise you'll always feel compromised. No one can make you feel inadequate without your own consent. It's easy to keep blaming other people for having an issue with money, when in fact all they are doing is reflecting some of your own anxieties over money issues. You are not worth exactly what you believe you are worth.

Personal Relationships

Many couples agonise, despair and suffer feelings of rejection when they discover that the object of their desires has thoughts, feelings, emotions and opinions far removed from their own. At the start of any relationship, you are mentally accumulating all the things you have in common that make you so compatible. For the most part, your partner retains all the questions that initially attracted you, and you spend the rest of the relationship dealing with the things you didn't notice at the beginning.

When you make a decision in your relationship, there are always consequences, but taking no action can result in long-term pain, whereas the pain caused by taking action is usually more short-lived.

No matter how much fear you have about dealing with something or making a decision, not dealing with it won't change things. In fact, not dealing with it may make things a whole lot worse. The relationship starts to become corrosive, and if you're not eating away at yourself, you'll find a way of directing your dissatisfaction at your partner.

Family

While it's natural to experience your own feelings of upset when a loved one is suffering, you have to take care not to overload them with your own pain. When you talk about your own pain to someone who is seeking support, it can get quite competitive and, once you get locked into your own pain, you become unavailable to support the other person.

Even when family bonds are very close, it is risky to assume that you can unload a problem on to the nearest person. But there are times when you need to stand back. You may be the one called on for support, and to fulfil that role, your own needs may have to be met elsewhere.

Respecting the opinion of another family member is important, and when it is clear that your view of a person is not shared, it may be appropriate to hold back. There are occasions when an individual is determined to pursue a particular line. There are usually plenty of warning signs when conflicts lies ahead, but still some people choose to ignore them. The biggest fights that take place are internal ones. No matter how unpleasant you think someone is, you can be sure that not everyone will see them in the same light. The bullying boss might be perfectly sweet to his wife and children. The office bitch might donate half her salary to charity, and always remember to telephone her mother.

There are always people that you choose not to have in your life. The difference with family is that you don't choose it, it's already in place. You can set your own boundaries, though, and you may have to respect those set by other family members.

Friends and Social Life

Friendships are often based on where you are at a specific moment in your life. So if you were to meet a friend through work, you may find that you have many common interests, but the overriding connection would be your mutual employment. If that connection is lost, those bonds can be broken.

Vested interests

When a friend has a vested interest in keeping you where you are, it may not be as sinister as it sounds. Many friendships depend on the playing out of familiar roles such as work relationship changes. You may be offering something different, which is not readily accepted by some. Equally, what they have to offer to you can become less appealing.

You could have a friend who always used to unload all their problems on you. After having read this book, you might start wanting to encourage change in them. The best way to absorb any technique fully is by teaching it to others. But sometimes, friends just want a sounding board and not a few forms to fill. If a friend simply wants you to listen and be supportive, you can still do that. But you will find it harder to give negative feedback. You are working on a programme now which will affect the way you think, act and communicate. You will communicate positively about other people and yourself.

Why would those who profess friendship abandon you when you decide to get your life in order? I have always been quick to preach the benefits of moving on in life, and not allowing other people's actions to detract from my own life's mission. Making the decision to change my life was certainly my salvation, and if it meant leaving certain people behind, well, so be it.

It's not like we're victims of a premeditated and personal attack. More often than not these people are more caught up in their own lives, and what's relevant to them at the time. The theory says that, at times in your life, you can act like a magnet to certain people. For whatever reason, you are offering the feedback or scenario that is attractive to them. Once you change what's on offer, the new offer is less appealing to them.

There may have been a time in your own life when you were stuck in a negative cycle, and a friend tried to pull you out of it. You may have sought the company of friends who you felt understood your dilemma, and had similar problems. When you're stuck in a negative cycle it feels comfortable having support. Once you decide to break that mould and move forward, you will see some friends in a different light. It's not just a case of some friends finding you less appealing: you may find yourself less attracted to them.

If you see friends as colours of the rainbow, you have the flexibility to allow for colour changes. You don't expect one friend to be all the colours: they each have something unique to offer. Perhaps on occasions you have expected too much from a friend, and have wanted them to be all the colours. We are all different things to different people and, at times, different things to the same people, so after all may be we don't have only one colour. As you move through various phases, so do your friends.

You may have good reason to discontinue a particular friendship, but that's not to say you have to close the door completely or be left with regrets. Staying positive means focusing on what was good, and if you reach a point when it's no longer good, you can still move on with positive memories. You don't know what the future holds, and you might have experienced friends moving in and out of your life at different times.

How good is your social life? Does it reflect you as a person? Some people are always busy, and have lots to do in their spare time. Life might be a round of endless parties, sporting activities and social gatherings. Some individuals keep themselves endlessly busy, because they hate spending time in their own company. Part of the quality time you allocate yourself should involve time alone. It allows you to reflect and recharge, and get your own thoughts in order, without having the constant input from others. Can you imagine going through life at a pace that twenty years of your life slipped by, and you never stopped to contemplate if you were doing something that made you happy? No matter how great the goals you achieve, it means little without personal satisfaction. Even if you have an action-packed social life, it will only benefit you if you are actually enjoying it.

When you plan your social life the emphasis has to be on quality time. Your social life should be reflective of you. This means reflective of the sort of person you really are, and not trying to fit into other people's perceptions. Social life requires time, and if you don't monitor your time it's soon taken up doing things you'd rather not be doing. So, have to plan for a social life, and make a commitment to it.

One of the problems of city life is that it's very transient and people tend to move around a lot. You can find yourself with a different group of friends every few years. What's really required is active participation on your part to generate a social life. Instead of waiting around to receive an invitation, you could be the one to initiate it.

You can use your file to gather information on forthcoming events and places of interest to visit. As a useful exercise, select four seasonal events for the year to look forward to. Once you've done that, you can break the year down into months, and make sure that you have at least one social treat planned each month. If you don't, it's so easy for the months to slip by, and you end up not doing anything you particularly enjoy.

How to Score One

I'm sure you have come across people who can talk a really good plan, but they never get round to implementing it. Many people get caught in the planning, they spend their whole life swamped in the finer detail, and are ultimately distracted from the final result because they never put any plans into action. You need to get involved in the doing, so you start living your goal, and not just dreaming it. This can involve you questioning your concept of what's in store for you in the future. If you are convinced that there is a good reason for not implementing a goal immediately, make sure you are still contributing to that goal. Opportunities have to be seized, and sometimes you have to jiggle with the sequence of events to make them happen.

Life has a wonderful way of surprising you. However far you think you have come there, is always a new challenge on the horizon. Each challenge you face takes place on a personal level. There is no universal scale of success, only your own levels of success. Every time it hurts, you know you are pushing yourself beyond your own boundaries. You will enjoy it in the process; that hill is worth climbing.

There is something phenomenally powerful about writing out your goals. The speed at which things can happen is breathtaking. Even when you believe what you are doing is right, and you feel passionate about it, you still have to overcome your own personal fears. If you hold on to that strength of feeling, you'll overcome your fears, and passion will be your driving force. Fear is like a splinter that gets under your skin, and if you don't get it out, it will start an infection and work its way into your whole system. So the minute you feel the prickly effects of those dreaded splinters, you must make a conscious effort to root them out.

It's not the most talented individuals who make it, but the most determined ones. Your goals are achievable: all it takes is for you to believe it, and you'll find a way to make them happen. The only thing that can hold you back, or limit you from realising your full potential is fear, so you have to learn to stop it infecting your passion. Use it to your advantage. If fear is telling you that you can't do something, go out and prove it wrong. Fill in your missing blanks. There is no real logic to your fear or accurate point of reference. Even if things didn't work out in the past, you are still faced with a new scenario that allows you to change the running order. It really is up to you. Once you start to use your brain to work out some tactical manoeuvres you'll get to whenever it is you want to go.

Some challenges and goals will feel uphill every step of the way. That's fine, because you are doing your groundwork in the process. There will be some development skills that seem to come amazingly easily. Others you will have to be patient about, but trust yourself: you will acquire them along the way. What's really important is the formula you are subscribing to.

How Changes Operate in your Personality

The changes that matter most are more often changes in perception than changes in the world outside us.

If you do virtually anything consistently for seven days it will change you. The actions you take will set up a wave of change in your life, that will in turn affect many other areas of your life, which in turn affect others. It becomes difficult to stop once it builds up sufficient momentum.

The human mind generalizes as a learning principle. For example, as a child you learn how a door opens and closes. Your mind then generalizes that learning to apply to all doors everywhere. This works equally well whether the learnings are useful or painful. However, you can dismantle many of the negative generalizations you have made about the world, and build positive ones.

Most people spend more time learning to work their DVD player, than they do with their own mind. Your mind can make you a happier, more confident and powerful person.

If you woke up one morning and your life had become exactly what you wanted it to be, what would you see? What would you hear? What would you feel inside? What changes would have happened in your career? In your relationships? Your finances? Your health?

Every time you play with these ideas, you've planting positive suggestions in your mind. If you work consistently with these ideas, your mind will generalize them and start acting accordingly, thus showing you where to find the right opportunities, situations, for the product of your imagination to become true.

It's like a virtuous circle of un-learning bad habits and learning new ones. Goodbye past! It won't happen overnight, it will start happening after a certain number of repetitions, like when your mind learned that 6 x 7 is 42. Do you remember how many times did you have to repeat that to yourself until it was finally engraved in your mind? Then you didn't have to think about it, as it became a second nature.

Whatever you achieve in the next ten years will be the result of what you do now – imagine, imagine, stop thinking, imagine!

Responsibility

Responsibility is about control. Do you want to control your life, or hand over that control to other people – your family, the media, or even society in general? It's easy to blame your parents, employers or the government for your problems, but until you decide to see yourself as responsible for your situation, then you don't have any power to change it.

Taking responsibility is not the same as taking the blame. You are not responsible for the hand you have been dealt, but it is always up to you how you play it.

Stop for a moment and imagine what it would be like to take responsibility for your life – to have the power to make choices and changes in every area of your life. To be in control of your finances, your relationships and your sense of well-being. To be at peace with those things that are not in your control and in full command of those that are. Make the decision right now to take responsibility for your life at a whole new level.

Brainwashing

Our behaviour is a direct result of the person we believe we are – our self-image. We are constantly confirming to ourselves that we are the person we think we are, but the system we use to interpret our behaviour and feedback is our own self-image. It's a Catch-22.

Your self-image is the way you see yourself in your imagination. The reason your self-image is so powerful, is because your behaviour will almost never deviate from this internal map. It acts as a sort of self-fulfilling prophecy, telling you how to behave or perform to act consistently with the kind of person you think you are. Yet many people don't even realise they have an image of themselves, until they look. If you truly believe you are unattractive, you will unconsciously sabotage any attempts to make yourself appear attractive. Because you won't represent yourself at your best, people will inevitably find you unattractive and the prophecy is fulfilled.

How you think of yourself, also affects how other people feel about you. Because 90 per cent of what we communicate is unconscious, the people around you are continually responding to your body language, tone of voice and the emotional signals you are transmitting. Even if the words you use sound positive, you may well find yourself conveying one message verbally, and a completely different message with your body language.

You are constantly letting other people know how to treat you by the way you treat yourself.

We settle in life for what we feel we are worth. We will never allow anyone to abuse us, more than we abuse ourselves.

Unfortunately, while each failure reinforces the self-fulfilling prophecy of your negative self-image, your outer successes rarely change it for the better. No matter how much you have on the outside – bigger house, bigger car, more money – it will not ultimately satisfy you if you don't already feel good about yourself on the inside.

A large number of people create an outer veneer as a way of hiding personal feelings of inadequacy. They project any number of things to compensate for a lack of inner self-worth, flaunting their wealth, status, intellectual achievement, physical strength, social connections, or moral 'superiority' in an attempt to prove that they are not as worthless as they feel inside. Over the years it develops into an entire outer persona that is the completely opposite of how they feel on the inside. They continually feel like a fraud, fearing that at any moment they are going to be 'found out' and it will all be taken away from them. Many people whom we consider in our culture to have everything are secret self-haters. The bigger the jewellery, the smaller the self-image.

While some of the earliest messages you got from your family were no doubt positive, many of them were not. In an average, parents criticize their children more times than they praise them.

At school, many people are bigger than you and seem to know more than you do. Teachers unwittingly de-genius you at school by their efforts to mould you. There are also people around you with low self-esteem, who covertly undermine you to make themselves feel better.

The reason you are not yet living the life of your dreams is that you are wasting so much of your time and energy hiding your negative self-image from the world.

Your authentic self, who you really are, cannot be heard when all your energy is going into maintaining the illusion of your projected self, and hiding the image of your feared self from the world.

The three selves

At our core is our authentic self. Piled on top of the real us is a layer of shame, fear and guilt, what we are afraid to be, our negative self-image. Yet we pile on top another layer – the person we pretend to be in order to be liked, to get love and money.

As you begin to excavate your real self out from under who you've afraid you are and who you pretend to be, you got to shift positions from driven to driver, and you get to have more ease, more fun and more you in your life.

The key programmes of human behaviour are habit and imagination, and they are far more powerful than logic and will power will ever be. Your body responds far more readily to the vivid use of imagination than to a simple command.

If you teach people who have a negative self-image to repeatedly imagine themselves as ideally they want to be, you'll notice they become happier and more at peace with themselves in a matter of days.

It is not how we like to think of ourselves, but whom we truly believe we are. Once we make a commitment, the rest of us aligns with it. All truly successful people accept their brilliance – they are not embarrassed by it. The better you feel on the inside, the better your life will become. You have a special gift of uniqueness to bring to the world.

Your internal representation of reality is unique to you – your own personal way of perceiving the world. It is your own map of the world, but it is incomplete and filled with generalizations, deletions and distortions ('the map is not the territory').

Everybody has the ability to visualize. Yet too many people exert more control over the movies they go to on the outside, than the movies they play in their mind.

As you learn to change the pictures and sounds in your mind, you too will get conscious control of your life.

Images that are bigger, brighter and bolder have greater emotional intensity than those that are duller, dimmer and further away.

To reduce the intensity, step out and move back; to increase the intensity, step in and make it bigger.

The way you feel from moment to moment is a direct result of the way you are using your body, and the picture and sounds you are making in your mind.

Nothing takes the wind out of your sails more quickly than a few critical comments, made by the wrong person at the wrong time. The worst critic you will ever encounter is the one who lives inside your mind. But criticism is meant to be constructive, positive, to stop you from making mistakes and help you do things better. You have a choice. You are in control.

The brain is a mass of millions of neural pathways, with each idea or memory moving along its own path. Whenever we do something new, we create a new neural pathways so we can re-access that experience again more easily. Each time we repeat a particular behaviour, we strengthen the associated neural pathway, just as when you walk down a path through a field it becomes a clearer path.

These neural pathways in the brain actually get physically larger through repetition of behaviour. That is how people become 'hard-wired' to certain automatic behaviours, such as smoking and overeating. We can design that same mental architecture to design pathways to success and happiness, and to create associations that allow us to 'switch on' certain feelings whenever we want them.

Charismatic people feel comfortable in themselves. Because they are content with who they are, they aren't desperately looking for the approval of others and they aren't trying to manipulate others into liking them. Ironically, that's why we feel drawn to them.

Emotional Intelligence

An emotion works like someone knocking on your door to deliver a message. If the message is urgent, it knocks loudly. If it is very urgent, it knocks very loudly. If you don't answer the door, it knocks louder and louder and louder until you open the door. Then it delivers its message. As soon as you understand even part of it, it becomes part of your self-understanding. You are changed, and the emotion has done its job.

To reach the wisdom of our emotions, we must work with them. Some of our thoughts are banal and meaningless; others are meaningful and worthwhile. It is the same with our feelings: some are trivial; some are profound. Learning to handle our emotions and to understand them is a fundamental part of growing up, just like learning to use our mind to think clearly, or using our hands to write or draw or make things.

How do I recognize emotions that have an important message I need to learn from? If an emotion is unimportant, or no longer truly relevant to your life, it vanishes when you change the pictures in your hand. If it is important and relates to a real, current situation that you need to learn from, it will come back again and again and again. In that case, when the emotion turns up you need to listen and learn from it.

The more often we repeat a pattern of behaviour, the stronger that pattern becomes. When we indulge in negativity over the years, we literally hardwire ourselves to be negative.

Positive perspective

Your experience of life is primarily affected by the perspective you view it from. Depending upon the meaning we give to situations or events, we will feel and behave differently.

Some people always manage to look at things in a positive way. They have an ability to frame any situation in a way that leaves them feeling empowered and strong (for these people, the glass is always half full rather than the reverse).

The meanings we attribute to the events in our lives are determined by the parts of our experience we choose to make important. Our interpretation of any situation depends on what we include or exclude from our frame of perception. The fact is: everything is relative. When you think one situation is bad, that is because you are comparing it to something you perceive is better. The advantage of being able to decide how you frame events, is that it gives you more choices. More choices gives us greater flexibility, and greater flexibility leads to an increased ability to influence the results in any situation.

Flexibility is power: the most powerful person in any group is invariably the most flexible. The individual who has the most ways of looking at things has the most choices, and hence the greatest possibility of controlling the outcome of any situation. The art of reframing the world with a positive perspective is not about ignoring problems, but about having sufficient flexibility to make your point of view work for you instead of against you.

Failure is an attitude, not an outcome. It's nothing to do with the results you produce and everything to do with how you frame things. Edison didn't fail thousands of times before being successful with the electric lamp, but he was eliminating all the ways that would not work. He succeeded in framing his particular challenge in a way that helped keep him motivated. He was flexible enough in his thinking to give himself more choices.

One of the most powerful framing tools we all use on a daily basis is also one of the simplest – the power of questions. Questions determine the focus of our perception, as well as the amount of success, love, fear, anger, joy or wonder that we experience on an ongoing basis. Questions direct your focus, and you always get more of what you focus on in your life. If your quality of life is poor, examine your inner questions and and ask yourself how more empowering you can make them. Start by asking questions that presuppose the positive; these questions make your brain sort for different information and put you in a different and more resourceful state. If you are not happy with the answer you are getting back, you can either change the question or keep asking until you are. Your brain will keep searching for you until a useful answer has been found.

The kind of questions Einstein particularly excelled at are 'possibility questions', questions that focus the mind on what is possible but may not have been considered before. You always get more of what you focus on in life. So it's vitally important to acknowledge and concentrate on your successes, great and small – on what's really healthy and rewarding around you.

The secret of getting on well with others is to be able to see the world through their eyes. Seeing from many perspectives gives flexibility in thinking and actions. People do what they do in order to achieve some purpose or fulfilling some need. Most people have a positive intention behind their behaviour, even when they are taking a position that seems contentious or contrary to our own best interests.

The power of belief

The most powerful frame we can use to shape our perspective, is what we choose to believe about ourselves and the world. Our beliefs can determine our level of intelligence, our happiness, the quality of our relationships, even our health and success. What we believe has a far greater influence on our life than objective truth. Beliefs are the windows through which you view the world. If your 'belief window' is covered with too much negativity, you will see a dangerous world filled with untrustworthy people. If you replace the beliefs on your window with positive ones, you get to live in a friendly world, where you are able to make smart choices.

Your beliefs determine your decisions, how you feel about things, and ultimately the direction you go in life. They control everything about you. What you perceive in the world is a manifestation of the beliefs you hold in your mind. Do you feel in control? Do you feel empowered? Do you feel exceptional levels of happiness most of the time?

Everyone does what they do for a very good reason, even though the reason may seem inappropriate to the outside world. If someone has a fear of flying, it might be for any number of reasons, but if we assume the phobia has a positive intent, we know it will probably come down to the desire to be safe. As your unconscious mind finds new ways of keeping you safe without the unnecessary phobic response, the phobia itself becomes unnecessary.

You already have all the resources you need to succeed. The difference between you and someone who is already living their genius, is learning how to access your resources at the appropriate times.

You can accomplish anything if you break the task down into small enough chunks. Any skill can be learned, and every problem solved, if it is broken down into small enough pieces. When you train your brain to look at huge tasks in terms of simple, achievable steps, the huge tasks become much more possible. If you want to knock down the wall between you and the life of your dreams, it's best to do it one brick at a time.

What feels normal to us is more a product of our programming than our potential. If you want to begin producing different results in your life, you'll need to step outside your comfort zone and do something different.

You have failed when you decide to stop learning. Until then, every response you get is valuable information. That can be used to tell you whether your actions are taking you closer to, or further away, from what you want. Success is what happens when you've done failing. The people who've 'made it' have made more mistakes than the people who haven't. Every mistake or failure is a learning opportunity in disguise. Failure is a requisite part of the learning process, not the end of the learning process. People don't fail – strategies, tactics and plans fail. Change them until you find one that succeeds. Fear of failure is a potent demotivator, but give yourself permission to fail at least ten times. In this way you'll lessen its emotional charge.

You are creating your future now. The difference between the people who succeed and the ones who struggle is whether they look into the past or the present to create their future. If you look to the present, you will always find there is some new choice you can make to enhance your possibilities.

Dream On

For anything to happen in the real world it first has to happen in the imaginary world.

In order for you to improve your life, yourself or the world, you first need to allow yourself to dream. When the mind has a target, it can focus and direct itself until it reaches its goal. If you have no targets, your energy is dissipated. Yet, what you achieve in your pursuit of success, is often so as important as who you become in the process. When you're working on a truly worthwhile dream, the dream is also working on you. Just as going to college isn't about getting a piece of paper, dream-setting is not just about getting what you want – it's about becoming more than you even thought you could be.

The most important things in the world

What would you do if the world was going to end one week from today? Your answer to that question is the key to identifying your values – those things that matter most in your life. The opportunities to live abundantly are all around us, but just acquiring the symbols of success will not make us any happier. When you learn to focus on your values, and your life's purpose, instead of just your goals, you will automatically begin to take the big picture of your life into account.

Jump ahead to the end of your life. What are the three more important lessons you have learned and why are they so critical?

Think of someone you respect and describe three qualities you admire.

Who are you at your best?

What one-sentence inscription would you like to see on your tombstone that would capture who you really were in your life?

Make a list of the most important things that emerged from answering these questions. Be sure to look beyond any material things on your list to the states of being which lie behind them.

Someone says that the most important thing in his world is money. When asked what having money would give him, he said feeling of security and respect. What was really important to him was security and respect – those were the states of being he was really pursuing, not money. Choose your top five values – the things on your list you absolutely cannot imagine going without. These five things are the very essence of what will give your life meaning – the most important things in your world.

If you do nothing else but live these values every single day, you cannot imagine how fulfilling your life will become.

Brainstorm

When it comes to your success, you need to become unreasonable. You need to have dreams that are beyond what you and everybody around you think of as possible. Make a list of everything you want now, have wanted in the past, or can conceive of wanting in the future.

Don't ask what the world needs – ask what makes you come alive, and then go and do that. What the world needs is people who have come alive.

- What do you love to do so much that you'd pay to do it?
- What do you feel really passionate about?
- What would you choose to do if you had unlimited resources?
- Who are the people or characters from history you most admire and why?

Answering these questions will help you to get an overall idea of what your life's purpose is about. It takes the limitations of your present mindset off, and lets you become outrageously creative.

- What did you want to do as a child?
- What did you want to be when you grew up?
- What would you do if you were guaranteed success?
- What would you really love to happen?
- What would you really like to learn?
- What skills do you want to master?
- How much money do you want to earn?
- What character traits do you want to develop?
- What do you want to give back to the world?

When you focus upon what you do want, as opposed to what you don't, you are making sensory-rich experiences of what you will see, hear, feel, taste, and smell when you get what you want. By regularly concentrating on what you do want, you will condition your mind to attract more of it to you.

Measuring success

One of the simplest keys to staying motivated over time is to give yourself every opportunity to experience an ongoing sense of progress in the pursuit of your goals. Instead of waiting until you have either achieved your goal or failed, continually look and listen for any sign of progress toward your goal; when you find one, grab onto it with all your heart. Seize on any evidence you can find that you are moving in the right direction and delight in it. Hold it large in your mind. More than anything else, it is this ongoing sense of progress that will keep you moving in the direction of your dreams, week by week and moment by moment.

- What will you see as you achieve your dream?
- What will you hear?
- What will you feel, smell and taste?

Your answers to these questions will give you a way of knowing if you are getting nearer to or further from your dreams, and will keep you motivated as you begin living the life of your dreams.

Whenever we do something new, we create a neural pathway so we can reaccess that experience again easily. Each time we repeat a particular behaviour, we strengthen the associated neural pathway. This is why it is so important to mentally rehearse success. Top athletes play hundreds of successful matches, and won thousands of races in their own minds, before setting foot on the playing field. As you visualize living your dream every day, you will build stronger neural pathways to success.

Taking action

By creating a vivid representation of how you ideally want to live your life and focusing on it everyday, you will become motivated to take action and you will know where you are going.

A journey of a thousand miles begins with a single step. Think of at least one thing that you can do today which will take you in the direction of living your dream, and do it, a phone call, a little bit of research. The moment you commit to something, providence moves too, and all sorts of unforeseen incidents and assistance occur. It's as though your commitment becomes a magnet for good things to be drawn to you.

Believe yourself well

We all have our own immune system: the body and the mind working together to heal, protect and regulate the vessel that we essentially are. Many people expect instant cures from the doctors for their ills, and hand over responsibility for their health to the medical profession, preferring a prescription to instigating a change in their lifestyle of diet.

Survivors of cancer share one essential trait: they believed that what they were doing would work for them.

A placebo is a tablet with no inherent curative properties. Placebos are about 30 per cent as effective as a medical drug. In some specific cases their effectiveness is much higher. We are only beginning to understand the incredible power of hypnosis, and its possible role in medicine and therapy in the future. Some doctors have recently proved how just using the imagination can affect your health. People who believe they can control their immune system, find that they can easily do so by using hypnotic or guided imagery techniques. Many individuals could actually increase the number of protective blood cells in their bodies almost at will, instantly improving their resistance to illness.

PsychoNeuroImmunology studies how it's possible to boost your immune system, just by thinking about it in certain ways. The idea behind PNI is that our body knows how to repair itself and maintain perfect holistic health. Programmed into your immune system is the ability to recognize those cells that belong to you, and those that are invaders from the outside, which must be destroyed or appropriately consumed. Once your immune system comes in contact with bacteria, a virus or an abnormal cell, it will never forget the encounter. During its first exposure, your immune system produces targeted 'biochemical weapons' designed to combat that specific abnormal 'invader'. Your immune system is strong and intelligent enough to control and coordinate its actions, so that you effortlessly maintain a state of healthy vitality.

Creating money

Real wealth isn't just about money – it's about your access to resources, whether or not those resources technically belong to you. Real wealth is about having an abundance of good health and true happiness. It's about having good friends or family, people who stimulate and fascinate you. Real wealth is feeling happy most of the time. It's a sense of contributing something to the world, and that your life is worthwhile. You are unique – nobody can do things exactly the way you do them.

Money is essentially a symbol of value, it represents value although it has no inherent value of its own. Money is a symbol of our confidence in our product, our service and ourselves. If you want to have more money in your life – for yourself or to help others or both –, then you have to make yourself more valuable in the eyes of other people. It won't be enough to provide valuable goods and services, or to be in the right place at the right time. You'll have to be more spiritual than that. You'll have to have more faith, more confidence, in your own value, as a provider or as a person. The more confidence we have in ourselves and / or our product or service, the more we will be able to change for it.

A massive proportion of those who get large sums of money from lotteries or inheritance, are almost guaranteed to lose it all very quickly. Eighty per cent are actually worse off financially just two years later. That's because inside they still feel poor. In Psychology, this is referred to as 'the Pygmalion effect' or the 'self-fulfilling prophecy'. What we expect to be true in our minds will tend to become true in reality. We act in ways that are consistent with our expectations. Those actions then create the results we expected, and the 'prophecy' or our expectations is fulfilled. If you believe you can't really become wealthy, you will speak and act consistently with that belief, and in most cases 'prove' yourself right. Similarly, if you change your expectations of the world to reflect your infinite potential for wealth, you will quickly generate the thoughts, feelings and behaviours that will draw money to you.

The Bible says 'the love of money is the root of all evil', not 'money is the root of all evil', that is, acquiring money for its own sake, as a commodity to be hoarded. If you believe money is bad in some way, you will unconsciously sabotage your attempts to create more of it in your life. Most wealthy successful people tend to share the same simple habits and beliefs about prosperity. Many people unknowingly use this same powerful principle to keep themselves poor, through the beliefs and habits they have towards money. Instead of taking responsibility for their beliefs and actions and therefore for their wealth, they use their lack of money as 'proof' that they are meant to be poor. They have affirmed their poverty over and over so many times that it unwittingly became a self-fulfilling prophecy, a poverty consciousness.

Law Making

In hypnosis, the idea called the Law of reversed effort can be summed up in the pop psychology phrase: What you resist persists. Some people have deep rooted beliefs that keep them poor. For one reason or another they sabotage themselves getting rich. No matter how hard they try consciously to get rich, their unsconscious beliefs will not support them and they end up sabotaging themselves. The Law of reversed effort teaches us that if deep down you think of yourself as poor, you'll constantly fear poverty. Since what you focus on you get more of, poverty is usually exactly what you'll get.

A concern for organized finances is not the same as a dread of poverty. But that deep-rooted fear of poverty is how some people manage to amass huge riches without ever getting out of the trap of poverty consciousness.

What you focus on consistently, you get more of in your life. If you focus on poverty and lack, you will tend to get more of that in your life. If you focus on the wealth that is already there, you will tend to get more. Those who focus upon the positive in life and attract it to them are called 'lucky'.

We can create our own luck. Many highly successful people choose to believe in the Law of attraction, this is one reason why rich people tend to associate with other rich people and why they get richer. Your thoughts are an energy that is both powerful and creative.

The principle of 'sympathetic resonance' says that you are always attracting people and circumstances that resonate with your predominant thoughts. It would be good to attune your mind to notice how many opportunities there are to become wealthier. Begin thinking of yourself as someone who deserves great wealth.

What would having more money give you that you don't already have?

If you answer happiness, freedom, security, power, money itself is not the source of any of these things. Each of these words represents a state you can generate within you, a neuro-chemical event in your body and mind. If money was really the key to happiness, freedom, security or power, people like Kurt Cobain, Elvis Presley, Marilyn Monroe or Whitney Houston would still be with us today.

Corollary to the Law of Reversed Effort:

If you want to get something in order to feel a certain way, feeling that way now will be the fastest way to get it.

You'll never meet a millionaire working for an hourly wage. If you want to create massive financial abundance, it is necessary to first recognize that your ability to make money is intimately linked to your ability to add, create and provide value, whether to a person, a project, a company or an enterprise. Money is one of the rewards you get for adding value to the lives of others.

Imagine you already have all the good feelings that being wealthy will bring you. All the happiness, all the confidence, and all the love you could ever hope for, is there inside you...

Imagine yourself going through your day. How do you treat people? How do they treat you? What are you especially proud of about today? What do you love doing? What do you do exceptionally well? What value have you added today? How could you add even more? Who else could you impact with your work? How about with your life?

There are two kinds of happiness. The one most of us think of is simply feeling wonderful in your body. The other, more subtle form of happiness is a state of being in perfect harmony with life, the universe and everything (what they call the flow, the groove, the zone).

In the West, our culture emphasizes the pursuit of happiness through external means.

In the East, traditional culture emphasizes acceptance of the conditions of existence, positing the idea that happiness is found within.

Happiness is not a result: it's a state of mind and body.

You already know how to create states, and you can learn to experience that state we call happiness.

Many people puts obstacles in the way of feeling happiness. While some people are still waiting for things outside them to 'make them happy', others are concerned about feeling happiness inappropriately. Happiness is first and foremost a choice.

There are thousands of people walking around, experiencing background happiness and flow, in all areas of their lives. Whenever you've experienced flow in the past, your unconscious mind has made a record of the psychological and physiological aspects of that optimum experience. This is because flow is a neurophysiological state: in other words, it is a set of electrical impulses in your brain and chemical changes in your body. Your mind and body have a multisensory recording of exactly how you make flow happen, of how you make that state.

What you need to do is get your unconscious mind to go on a search, and find all the times in the past when you've experienced flow, then make a record of the state so that you can begin to trigger it for yourself more and more.

After a while almost anything you do can become effortless and joyous. You'll be doing something and you won't know why you feel so good, or why you are so harmoniously involved with what you are doing, and it will happen more and more.

One of the best ways to re-access flow is by remembering a time when you were in 'the zone', 'in flow'. Remember that the human nervous system cannot tell the difference between a real and a vividly imagined experience. All you need do is remember a time you were in flow and amplify it. If you do this each day, it will programme your mind and body to take you into 'the zone' more and more, able to say the right things in just the right way at the right time, easily thinking of the perfect thing to do, gliding through your days with an amazing sense of satisfaction.

Ask your unconscious mind to trigger that flow state throughout the day. As you begin to find yourself experiencing flow more and more of the time, the neural pathways in your brain will create flow and background happiness become stronger and stronger until you hard-wire yourself to be in flow all the time.

Pleasure

Pleasures are those things that feel good in the moment, that give the body pleasant sensations.

Satisfactions are those things that we feel good about afterwards, and gratify the soul.

The problem with pleasure is that it is so good, we can be easily be tempted to put it at the top of our priority list, as we pursue the good life at all costs. But pleasure pursued for its own sake, actually seems to get in the way of happiness. If you want to be happy, you need to take on a worthy challenge.

More than ever, the mind is now the dominant creative force on this planet. Our thoughts are more powerful than they ever have been, and with the exponential enhancements in technology, we are likely to see some amazing changes in the near future. We stand, many of us unknowingly, on the edge of an amazing leap in humanity's evolution. To make this leap, we need a radical shift in our values. Rather than continually looking for fulfilment in the outside world, which has made us overly competitive and selfish, we need to begin to find more contentment within. These days, a country's wealth is no longer gauged by its physical resources. Instead it is ideas and their implementation that create wealth. The real source of wealth is in our minds, and those of us with the richest ideas will create the greatest wealth in the world. You possess one of the most valuable and powerful pieces of equipment in the world right between your ears.

As you practise the teachings you learn, taking responsibility for programming your own mind, you are putting yourself at the forefront of our culture. You are becoming a leader, and the choices you make about where and how you lead, will become increasingly significant.

Discovering the values that motivate you

You sometimes do things for the strangest of reasons. Factors that seem to be strong motivators for you, such as the pursuit of money, can turn out to be empty and shallow as you realise that you really wanted more time. The word motivation stems from the Latin for movement, motivus. All change requires movement, so along with your beliefs (which can either propel you forward or hold you back) your motivation is one of the most important elements of your coaching journey.

Motivation can be defined roughly as what makes people tick. Motivation is different for everyone. You can't predict what works for any one individual, unless you really know the mix of needs and values that drive that individual, and the priority they allot to those needs and values. Your individual motivation is as unique to you as your fingerprints.

Certain behaviours are recognisable styles shared by certain groups of people. But you can choose to adapt and flex all of the behaviours to create the unique person that you are. You can apply the same principle to your motivation.

Knowing what your needs are

The first stage of creating your motivation map is recognising your emotional needs; the things you feel you must have to make you happy in some way. Some of your basic emotional needs may be:

- To be loved
- To be safe, secure, and certain
- To comfort and please your senses
- To feel special and important
- To experience new things

You also have 'higher' needs that make you feel good and may also benefit others or develop you in some way:

- To make forward progress in your life
- To make a difference in the world

Meeting some of these needs all of the time can be a tough trick to pull off, and may come at a price. Your need to feel loved may make you try so hard to please people, that you fail to stand up for your own best interests. Your need for safety may stop you from trying new things. Your need to feel special and important may drive you to seek out a promotion at work that ends up making you miserable. Your need to experience new things may result in you cheating on your partner out of boredom, after many years of marriage.

Your higher needs – making progress and making a difference – are more likely to result in overall good results for you, yet even here, when they are combined with more basic needs in the wrong way, they can have undesirable consequences. Imagine that you have a strong need to make a contribution to your community, so you volunteer your time and talents in a local charity. Imagine also that you have an even stronger need to feel special and significant. Perhaps you throw your weight around at committee meetings and this creates upset and disharmony in the group. The good that you do isn't cancelled out, it's just that there may be other, less pleasant results for you and other people because of the way you feel you need to behave, to get the notice you think you deserve. The trick is recognise what drives you, and ensure that your needs are met in ways that fit with your values. You're entitled to have needs, you need to find ways of meeting your needs that are life enhancing, not destructive, and sometimes you'll let go of needs that hold you back from being your best self.

Getting clear on your values

Your values are the principles that are most fundamental to you. Your values do link into your needs, yet they can be independent of them. Your values truly steer your motivation in a forward direction. You can have a strong need to feel loved that drives you to tell little white lies to your friends, when the honest truth is far kinder, but may cause them to be upset with you.

Some of the values that you hold may be:

- To be compassionate
- To lead and inspire
- To experience and create joy
- To love and be loved
- To be the best you can be
- To make a contribution to the world
- To provide for your loved ones
- To leave a legacy for people to remember you by
- To create wealth

Some values appear to be on the list of needs too. However, values and needs have a subtle difference. A true value generates positive forward motion, helping you to enjoy your life and develop yourself, and may also allow you to benefit those around you or the world in general. Think about the pleasure you get when you sit and watch TV passively for several hours. Sometimes you need it to comfort, relax, and amuse you – but it doesn't usually open up your horizons much. On the other hand, watching a challenging film or reading a book that fascinates you, often helps you to feel that you're more fully engaged with your world. You feed your value of growth or self-development.

Meeting only your needs can sometimes take you further into yourself, so that you may behave in a more selfish way. When you're living a life that is in tune with your values – no one else's – you often find that you're in harmony with the world around you. When everything in your life is in synch with your values, you enjoy yourself so much that you want everyone else to be as happy as you are. And being motivated to make that happen feeds your happiness even more. A virtuous circle!

Living up to your own values isn't always a bed of roses, but you'll find a world of difference between the discomfort that accompanies being true to yourself, and the pain that goes with avoidance. Some types of depression may be caused by avoiding living to your values – in depressing your instinct to be truly yourself, you cause a physical depression, which can be your mind and body telling you to step up, and take notice of your true values.

Which values give you a sense that your life is complete? A perfect life may in fact fail to make you happy. A life where you feel fully yourself, where you are making progress, and where you are contributing in some way to your world, may be perfect for you.

What are the things that you want to do, that you are excited about doing, and that you don't need to procrastinate on, because you can't wait to get going?

Your life changes whether you want it or not. Choosing to stand still means that in fact you go backwards, because your world changes around you. And when your world changes, even in small ways, you eventually get dragged along, sometimes kicking and screaming because not everyone embraces change. Just recognising that change is inevitable can be a relief. Putting yourself in control of the changes makes the journey a lot more enjoyable.

Asking for advice very definitely has its place. The problem is that advice, however well intentioned and wise, sometimes makes your dilemma worse. Advice can increase your confusion, make you doubt your own certainties, and can be even plain wrong. Until you get used to taking advice from yourself from that part of you that knows the answers, other people's opinions always have the potential to throw you off track. Really listening to yourself enables you to make quicker and more effective decisions.

Balancing assets and liabilities

Think of yourself and your life as a business, with assets and liabilities. Assets add value, and appreciate over the years. Liabilities are those things that come at a cost, and tend to deplete you over time. No business runs without liabilities, but a healthy company is rich in assets, and manages its liabilities. Some of your assets you already know, because they represent the things that are important to you, your true values. But seeing only the positive side of the balance sheet isn't going to get you where you want to be.

Redefining success

Your definitions of both success and failure change with time, experiences, and circumstances. What may have been a major failure in your early 20s may in fact have been the catalyst you needed to change jobs and really find your professional niche. 'There is no such thing as failure, or success, only a result or outcome from which we can learn.'

When nothing that you do matters, the only thing that matters is what you do. This adage is quite liberating. You have very little real control over how the world responds to your actions. You can in fact only have control over the integrity of your intention, the action that you then take, and your response to situations or events. Success is getting what you want; happiness is wanting what you get.

Tapping into your intuitive self

Curiosity is a wonderful thing to have, as you develop supporting awareness. You can take curiosity to a new level by taking steps to find out how intuitive you are, and how powerful intuition can be. Everyone has intuitive powers. Mostly you pick up evidence through your five senses – you consciously notice the clues in how you feel, and what you see, hear, touch and taste. But have you ever had that 'aha!' moment when your conscious mind is distracted and suddenly, out of nowhere, you get a new insight that helps you solve a problem. Trusting your instincts, living with a light touch, and tapping into the power of relaxed focus are some of the most effective ways to become more intuitive.

Living with a light heart

Life can be a serious old business at times, but taking every little setback to heart drains your energy. Laughter is truly one of the best medicines. Your brain works more efficiently when the negative emotions of worry and anxiety aren't weighing you down. Share a laugh or joke with colleagues, catch up with friends at the end of a busy day.

Sometimes the things you thought you really wanted turn out to be not so wonderful after all, which can be confusing.

You don't have to have what you've always had. You are not your past, as you are not your future. If you dwell on the past you tend to rely on your past experiences too much to make your decisions. That's like saying that 10 years ago you drove a Ford Fiesta, with limited speed and power capability, and now you own a Ferrari but still drive it like a Ford Cortina. You've acquired skills, learned lessons, gathered wisdom – you're capable of more than you achieved in the past. What you really want in your life now may have changed dramatically from old goals. If you neglect to question yourself about this, you can easily end up following an old pattern.

The action you take in the here and now creates the many possible futures that can exist for you.

Achieving what you really want depends on creating some kind of vision for yourself that you can begin to shape into tangible goals with a clear route to reaching them.

Money, Wealth and Abundance

Money and wealth aren't necessarily the same thing. Wealth issues usually centre on the degree of basic financial security you have, the extent to which you can live the lifestyle you want, and the provision you're making for the future. If you focus on what you want to have, do, and be in your life, and arrange your financials around those goals, you may well find that the money then flows far more easily than those times when you put the money cart before the wealth horse.

Most people have to work hard to develop a relationship with money that works well for them. If you live in the western hemisphere, you are already rich by the standards of developing countries. When you've acquired the latest car, phone or computer, you may feel encouraged to set your sights on the bigger, better, and newer version within a very short space of time. Discontent sets in very quickly, if your definition of feeling wealthy is tied into the acquisition of material things.

Perhaps the simplest way to avoid being happy in life is to compare yourself with other people (who are probably comparing themselves with you and getting the same effect). Such comparisons are at their sharpest and most painful in the realm of money and material possessions. You can easily get blinded by the shiny results of having money, and forget what you need it for in the first place.

Not having enough money can cause you anything from mild frustration to extreme distress, yet the pursuit of money for its own sake can have equally undesirable consequences, and may cloud or dilute the enjoyment you get from the things that are truly important to the success of your life.

Wealth is very different from money. You usually can't feel wealthy without first feeling that you have enough money, and entering the realms of the abundant is definitely trickier if you haven't fully defined the role of money and the meaning of wealth in your life.

Being financially secure

The constant worry that you may lose your financial security can hold you back from fulfilling your dreams, and not fulfilling your dreams can in turn stop you from generating the wealth and ultimately the security you most want and deserve. You can avoid this vicious circle by putting in place your own lifetime strategy that allows you breathing space and the knowledge that you can always survive financially, no matter what's round that corner.

Living your Chosen Lifestyle

No matter how much you enjoy your work, you probably hold the belief that you'd rather be enjoying more leisure time. You look forward to eating out in nice restaurants, or playing a round of golf, or lazing by the pool – and often these activities really do enhance your life. Sometimes though, your leisure pursuits don't give you what you expect. You may have occasionally experienced that flat feeling when you're on holiday, surrounded by the good things in life, willing yourself to have fun but in reality bored, restless, and discontented.

Your lifestyle is an aspect of your wealth; you may need money to enjoy a certain lifestyle, but your enjoyment of your lifestyle doesn't have to be directly related to how much money you spend. If you choose wisely and build a lifestyle that connects with what fires you up inside, your leisure time is well spent and pays dividends, creating a feeling of richness to your life. If you focus on things that 'should' make you happy but never really fully engage with them, true wealth doesn't get a chance to grow. You feel empty and cheated. Think hard about your leisure pursuits and the money and time you spend on them. Perhaps you shell out your hard-earned cash on a gym membership that you never use. A weekly run in the park with your best friend would do the job of getting you fit just as well, while feeding the inspiration and energy you get from your friend's company.

Like all tangible resources, money is not usually unlimited. If you fall into the trap of believing that the more money you spend on immediate gratification the happier you'll be, you end up being disappointed. And you'll deplete the financial resource that could be directed to areas to enhance your happiness. You can probably remember the thrill of your first really big-ticket purchase – a car, a down payment on a house, a holiday abroad – but the truth is, you get used to things. That thrill may have been a little less intense with the second car, the third house move, or the fourth exotic holiday. You may feel that you need to spend even more money to recapture that thrill. Consider what you lose out on, or jeopardise, by choosing the lifestyle that you have. Or perhaps you need to face up to the fact that money, and what it can buy, is pretty important to you and start to put strategies in place to attract more money into your life. Sometimes material possessions don't make up for the lack of a loving relationship in your life, and you may decide to direct some of the energies you currently place in creating money wealth into securing relationship wealth. Peace of mind concerning money issues often comes down to knowing where to direct your resources, and when to recognise that 'retail therapy' is often just a sticking plaster.

Permitting yourself to be rich

What assumptions about money do you hold? You may hold beliefs that stop you from generating the wealth you deserve. Do you think being poor is virtuous? You can find some pretty mean-spirited poor people out there as well as some wildly generous and philanthropic multimillionaires. Do you think you don't deserve to be wealthier than you are? What cash price do you put on yourself that limits you? Or do you think you don't have the talent, the commercial acumen, the persistence, or the drive to go out there and seek a glittering prize? Where is the evidence for your belief and what contrary evidence do you have? Where do your beliefs about money come from?

Cultivating a Feeling of Wealth and Abundance

Feeling wealthy in your life because you have developed a range of resources (cash and otherwise) is a great goal to aim for, and like all big goals, you need to keep focused on it. When you begin to feel wealthy (as opposed to simply well off) in your whole life, you can think about the next level – tapping into the abundance that you can create for yourself and your world.

Abundance means not only that you have all of these things in the proportion that is right for you, but you have a feeling of plenty in your life. You have enough, in fact more than enough, and have a sense of wanting to share out the money, time and love. You start feeling that you are been given more that what you give.

Giving away your resources of time, talents and/or money simply out of a spirit of generosity and goodwill, can often result in huge dividends in the form of personal satisfaction and fulfilling your sense of purpose. Yet you must accept that people may take advantage of you, and leave you feeling depleted and bruised. If you reduce your reliance on the return, generosity and goodwill will more easily flow back your way, directly or indirectly. You can cultivate abundance in many ways, big and small.

Don't devaluate yourself or your time. False modesty doesn't have a role in abundant lifestyle, and isn't helpful. If you're self-employed you must set a fair price for your labour and be confident that you're giving value to receive it. Abundance means that you can be generous when you've met your essential financial needs.

You can only cultivate abundance if you already have a strong sense of your wealth. You can only give out your precious resources of time and talent when you have first given them to yourself and to those dearest to you, and have amassed a surplus of energy that you actively want to pass on for the good of others. Being abundant, without taking care of the basics for you, won't always make you happy, and may even make you feel resentful.

Creating a relationship with yourself

When it comes to relationships, the only constant you have is the relationship that you build with yourself. Family members and friends may not always be there for you; you may never find 'the one', or you may be together for a while and the separate. Your children grow up and your relationship with them may change. Your wider networks may not always support you. You can deal with all of this and you can accept that everything changes over time – as long as the certainty of your self-esteem remains.

If your self-esteem is strong, you're comfortable in your own skin, and you don't feel the need to fill your time alone with distractions that may not enhance the overall quality of your life. If you don't manage to develop self-esteem, no matter how hard you try to please the important people in your life – and sometimes because of your efforts – you often find that real connection with them remains just out of your grasp.

Self-esteem means that you feel secure about your place in the world and the challenges you face, even when they're tough. Self-esteem may equate to self-confidence certainly, yet self-confidence in itself is often tied in some way to external factors such as the approval of a partner, or good feed-back from a boss. Building reserves of quiet self-esteem is far more beneficial for you than any quick-fix boost of confidence. Real self-esteem comes from a mixture of healthy respect for yourself and a mature understanding of your role in the world. The pillars of self-esteem are:

Finding your soul mate

If you're meeting your own needs and building your own self-esteem as a single person, finding a soul mate becomes a much less anxious pursuit. You're already presenting your best self to the world, which is naturally attractive and gives you the best chance of finding someone who is attracted to the real you. When you have high self-esteem, you can make relationship choices that feel healthy and mature. You don't fall prey to flattery or insincerity that feeds your vanity, and you can enjoy each other's company without wondering if this is 'the one' relationship to bring you happiness – because you're already happy. An ideal of romantic love or Mr or Ms Right won't give you something that you don't already have or can't get elsewhere. (Happiness is something you enjoy inside yourself, whatever the external circumstances.)

Biology may be partly to blame for the path of true love rarely being smooth. Human beings can be biologically attracted to people with opposite qualities and style to themselves, as nature attempts to mate two halves of a whole for the greater protection of future offspring. In the first flush of romantic love this dynamic is exciting and enjoyable, but over time these differences can be the very things that cause tension and disharmony. Check yourself for more detail on how to assess your own and others' personal preferred styles.

Building productive networks

Your wider networks are unique to you, and taking time to build productive relationships with people outside your immediate circle of close friends and family can really pay off. The more people you have access to in a positive, mutually beneficial relationship, the more support you have when you need it. Not everything you want to accomplish in your life is within your power to complete alone, no matter how self-sufficient you are. If information is power, other people often hold the information you need.

Widening your circle of influence

Your circle of influence contains all the people you have contact with in your life, from those who are closest to you, to your casual acquaintances. You touch or influence the lives of all of these people in some way and they do the same for you. Consider for a moment the areas where your circle of influence is already extensive. Perhaps you already make the effort at work to get to know people in other departments or divisions, or you're particularly good at building relationships with customers and suppliers. Do you maintain personal contact with some of these people when you move on from that job or do you invest all of your energies in a new circle of people? You have a limited store of time and energy so it may be impossible and unrealistic to stay in touch with everyone, but you may be able to keep in contact with a few key people who you've established rapport and respect with. How can you continue to benefit from their influence and support over the years?

What about your neighbours? Communication breakdown with neighbours can lead to painful disagreements and strained relationships that become difficult to repair. How satisfied are you with the quality of your connections with your neighbours? What opportunities do you have to play a bigger role in your community, perhaps at a local school, a neighbourhood watch group, or a social club?

Networking – the process of meeting new people and adding them to your circle for mutual benefit – isn't just for finding business opportunities. You can apply networks skills to any new social situation – a party, a fundraising event, or chatting to other parents.

Your mental and emotional wellbeing

Research on happiness suggests that 20 per cent of what makes us happy in life comes from personal characteristics such as our outlook on life, flexibility, openness to change, and resilience. Do you feel comfortable expressing your emotions, or do you bottle things up only to find they explode at just the wrong moment? Do you notice what your emotions are all the time, or do you find you sometimes feel upset but don't know why?

Non-violent communication advocates speaking from the heart in all interactions. Doing so helps you to become more assertive, to say what you really mean and need, in a factual way that doesn't threaten other people. The starting point is working out what your heart feels. Think of how you feel when your needs are being fulfilled – glad, joyful, proud, inspired, motivated, amazed, eager, thankful. Now think about how you feel when your needs are not being fulfilled – angry, frustrated, puzzled, annoyed, lonely, bitter, disappointed. The more specific you can be in identifying what you're actually feeling, the clearer you can be in expressing what you need out of a situation, and move yourself to a more positive emotion.

Recognising your emotions is half the battle. Expressing them in a way that gets the message across clearly and moves the situation forward in a positive way, is the next step to healthy emotional wellbeing. Think about the last time you were in a heated argument with someone close to you. Did you say – and hear – things that were hurtful and hard to forgive? In a calmer mood you realise that you didn't really mean some of what you said. Although getting things off your chest is good, letting strong emotion exaggerate the drama of a situation is rarely helpful. Take the sting out of arguments by staying mindful of what your needs really are. Perhaps you feel neglected or frustrated in a relationship. Choose to express yourself by describing the specific reasons that make you feel that way. Help the other person by explaining what action they can take to resolve matters. Don't forget to celebrate your happy and positive emotions. You can make a big impact on your emotional wellbeing by simply noticing the things that make you feel good, and going out of your way to make sure they're part of your life. Those mornings when you wake up full of enthusiasm for no particular reason don't come out of nowhere. If you can work out what those triggers are, it's like bottling up your own personal happiness formula for your future use.

Emotions release chemicals in your body that directly affect your physical state. Worry and anxiety can produce symptoms such as a dry throat, clammy palms, and feelings of nausea that often serve to make a difficult situation worse for you. You can affect your physical body by switching your thoughts, and you can change your emotional state by altering your physical state.

Everyday emotional health stems from your level of mental resilience and how quickly you can bounce back from setbacks. People are a lot less open about emotional and mental instability than they are about physical illness. Spotting the signs of stress that can lead to depression or physical illness is the first step towards dealing with the problem. What gives you mental strength? If you're living the life you want and are in control of what you are doing, you're likely to feel strong and resilient. What drains you mentally and how can you reduce the impact of this?

Developing and growing

The conscious changes you make not only give you better results; they help you grow as a person. In fact you constantly need to find new ways to grow, adapt, and change, otherwise your enjoyment of life over time can diminish, because you become used to the status quo.

Learning is simply a cycle of assessing information, making decisions, taking action and reflecting on your results to take better steps next time. Accelerated learning means you employ the strengths of both the left and the right sides of your brain

Being your best

Is it really important for you to aim to become competent at everything you do, to stay at that stage, and to enjoy the fruits of your labours? A higher level is always ahead and, sooner or later, if you want to grow to become your best self, you have to come to terms with letting yourself become incompetent on a regular basis – allowing yourself to struggle to move forward again at the higher level. What stages are you at?

The choices you make, and the actions you take, determine the results you get in life, and your choices and actions stem from how you think and use your brain power. You naturally develop preferences that work well most of the time, so you may not see the need to stretch yourself. Unless you change how you think, you continue to get pretty much the same results as you always have, because you probably choose the same actions and behaviours.

Having a strong sense of self enables you to handle even the worst events, and you begin to learn the truth in the saying 'what doesn't kill you makes you stronger'. You create your world through what you choose to focus on and do.

Achieving balance

Having balance means that you have a sense that all the parts of your life form a harmonious whole. You may work long hours, but if that produces your desired rewards, and allows you enough time to enjoy some leisure pursuits, then you're likely to feel balanced and stable. When you're off-balance, on the other hand, the smallest thing, such as an unexpected deadline, can send you over the tipping point – when things get overwhelming and you lose your balance point.

Simply trying to stand firm and hoping that you can keep all those plates spinning isn't really going to work for long, because something is sure to come along, knock you over, and send the plates crashing to the ground. The key to balance is to be in control of yourself and your goals, to keep moving in a forward direction, and yet to accept that sometimes you need to take a backwards or sideways step to maintain your momentum.

Finding your balance

Your sense of balance changes with your life priorities; you may be prepared to put lots of energy into your work and social life when you're a young adult because it may be very important to you to prove yourself, to earn the money you want, and to have fun. In your forties and beyond you may well have achieved a lot of your material goals, and find you want to spend more time rediscovering yourself, and trying out new things.

You may find that you make changes and adjustments, and things don't improve. You may actually miss the adrenaline rush and sense of achievement you got from work before. Think hard about whether you have too much or too little of something in your life. You may love the role of the giver in your social group, but feel that you 'ought' to be more assertive and less willing to drop what you're doing for a friend in need. Be honest about what you want and don't want in your life.

Where is your tipping point? Think back to days when you felt out of balance and identify your external and internal triggers.

Making the most of your leisure time

The habits you get into during your leisure time have a lot of impact on how much you enjoy your life as a whole. Your perfect vacation may be lazing by the pool – but check your assumptions once in a while. What's the best holiday you've ever had and why? Do you go back to the same resort or have a similar holiday every year because that's what feeds your soul, or because that's become a habit? Do you find that you need or want to take longer and longer to recharge? Do you find that a week or so of inactivity leaves you feeling less, not more, energised? Your lack of energy may have another explanation. Do you know people who never seem to stop doing things? They take on numerous projects at work and at home, and then spend their holidays learning to sky-dive or climbing minor mountain ranges. Sometimes, the more you do, the more energy you have. Look closely at your leisure time and see how you can get the best of both worlds, relaxing and action packed. If you usually holiday with your family, consider taking a solo short break, to reconnect with your own sense of self.

Your leisure time is a great opportunity for personal growth, as well as a blissful place where you can 'simply be' for a while, before you get right back into action.

Assessing your True Potential

Many people carry with them through life a nagging sense of wasted potential. They either undervalue their talents, or fail to appreciate what can be achieved through persistent effort and learning. There is no law, however, that condemns people to life in a rut. It is never too late to begin anew.

Everyone has talents, and with work it is entirely possible to make the most of your potential. Everyone possesses unused potential, and the first step is self-knowledge. Knowing yourself is also the first step toward any form of self-improvement. If you can make an accurate assessment of your aptitudes, your aspirations, and the strengths and limitations of your personality, then you will be in a strong position to really take charge of your life.

You can enhance your social skills and improve your ability to analyse your relationships. You can acquire missing personality qualities such as confidence of manner or improved sensitivity to the people around you. You can learn to be warmer and more relaxed in your interactions with people at home and at work. You can also train yourself to be more receptive to the nonverbal messages conveyed by body language, which often provide the most reliable guide to what people are actually thinking or feeling.

Many people complain in a generalized way about the quality of their lives, but they never stop to figure out exactly why they are discontented. It is better to identify the problems. Any plans that you make for turning things around in the future may prove futile, unless they are firmly grounded in a realistic appraisal of your current situation.

Another question that you have to ask yourself is whether any aspects of your own personality might be hindering your progress toward a better life.

Find where your personal strengths and weaknesses lie. There are common stumbling blocks on the path toward self-improvement. Anything from fears and inhibitions to a simple inability to express yourself could be preventing your fulfilment.

Step Back

Step back for a moment from your routine of work, home life, and social activity, and take a hard look at what you are doing, and where your life is headed. Most people have at least a vague sense that they could improve their lives. Does it sound like you? Most people are so deeply caught in the well-worn patterns of their daily existence, that they cannot even see the possibility that there may be alternatives.

Consider the place that work occupies in your overall scheme of things. Some people become enriched or fulfilled through their work, other people work primarily for the sake of the pay-check. For them, fulfilment lies in other activities, such as caring for their families or pursuing hobbies. By establishing your priorities, you can set specific goals that will move you toward achievement and self-improvement.

Before you can define your priorities, you need to form a clear picture of the kind of future you want. This exercise requires imagination, along with a grounding in reality. There is room for growth in your life, if only you can identify the areas that are ripe for development.

Is your life okay?

It is natural for human beings to strive for happiness and fulfilment. You could be part of the group of individuals who have successfully reappraised their lives, liberated themselves from old constraints, and as a consequence become much happier.

True happiness should not be confused with a state of stolid complacency. People need to develop their potential to the full. It is not enough merely to control your ego, and adjust as best you can to your social environment. You do not want to cut yourself down to fit the proportions of the life that you are living. Better to expand the scope of your life. Greater self-esteem and happiness can only come from a wider development of your individual capabilities. That is why it is so important to identify your hidden abilities, and map out a program for developing them and bringing them out into the open.

Even if you don't know the direction in which you should be going, it is a good principle always to expose yourself to new experiences and activities. When you find something interesting, repeat the experience and look for ways to develop it further. There is a good chance that this will lead to other new experiences, and to people with whom you would like to become involved.

Do you worry that you are not in the right job?

Doubts may arise when your confidence is low or when you are finding diminished satisfaction in your work. Psychologists place tremendous importance on the role that work plays in shaping a person's sense of status and achievement.

Self-knowledge

'Know thyself', the philosophers have counselled since ancient times. To attain self-fulfilment, you must first understand who you are, how you act, and what you want out of life. To understand yourself, you must piece together not only the obvious aspects of your personality, but also those that have been hidden from view.

You need to find out to what degree you are either introverted or extroverted, whether you tend to be stable or overemotional, or whether your whole approach to life is too tough or too tender, and you will be able to pinpoint both positive aspects of your personality that you may want to develop further, and destructive tendencies that may prevent you from achieving happiness. You will look at how you cope with anger and frustration, and characteristics you will wish to alter. Although your characteristics may not be immutable, your personality is.

The Roles You Play

Just as professional actors prepare for their performances, you learn to play different roles in everyday life – the conscientious employee, authoritative boss, devoted parent, playful lover, entertaining friend. The social roles you play can be a source of deep frustration, if they leave unexpressed large areas of your personality or abilities.

Alternatively, a deliberate decision to change the way you act – to present yourself to other people as more friendly or more assertive, for example – can lead to a positive change in the way that you are perceived.

Masked Emotions

Society encourages people to present a happy, smiling face to the world. Perhaps this is not a bad thing, but it is also important to share unhappy or negative emotions when they threaten to overwhelm you.

Frank talk about your emotions is not without its pitfalls. By opening yourself up to other people you risk putting yourself at a disadvantage, but if sharing your confidence inspires the other person to return the favour by confiding in you, both of your remain on an equal footing. Self-disclosure generally takes time and progress in small steps, with every step reciprocated by the other person.

Throughout history man has chosen the road of concealment rather than openness – a route that all too often results in sickness, misunderstanding, and alienation. If you conceal information about yourself, the people close to you are forced to read your mind and guess your needs. Through letting down your barriers, you not only gain a deeper self-understanding but you also enhance the quality of your intimate relationships.

Only if you are able to express all kinds of feelings can you expect to receive love in return. Mutual exchanges of intimacies will greatly enhance your feelings of security, trust, and confidence – all of which are vital for a successful relationship. By revealing your vulnerabilities and, where necessary, expressing your negative emotions, you can make others more thoughtful about your personality and your needs.

What is (and is not) Exceptional

Some people fail to make the most of their lives, or to achieve their most cherished ambitions, simply because they doubt that they are bright enough or sufficiently talented to secure their goals. In fact, all people have reserves of undeveloped skills, talents and resources waiting to be explored. Leonardo da Vinci and Albert Einstein achieved what they did, not because they were born with exceptional brains, but because they were able to make use of more of their total brain power than most people manage to do. Not everyone can be a genius, but the fact remains that people are capable of improving the skills that they possess, and even of developing new abilities in areas that are totally new to them.

Even if after self-examination you find – as most people do – shortcomings in your natural abilities, learn to regard your weaknesses as unexploited areas of potential ability warning to be unleashed. Then put your brain to work.

Everyone has access to the vast potential of the human brain. It is more powerful than any computer, and far more complex than any machine.

The brain's untapped potential

At birth, we each have our own maximum complement of brain cells. We lose many along our lives, but we know that the brain never loses its ability to acquire new skills. Without any particular effort on your part, your brain constantly records new memories. You may take up a new hobby, learn a new sport, or study a foreign language.

It is not the total number of nerve cells our brain possess that is important, but rather the number of new connections that nerve cells continue to make with one another. Scientific evidence suggests that when nerve cells are activated, they undergo changes that enable them to form firmer and more numerous bonds with other nerve cells. It seems that as long as your brain remains stimulated, nerve cells continue to increase their capacity for cross-communication, no matter what your age is. Attempt to acquire new skills, expose yourself to a wide variety of experiences.

Social contact is also important. Interacting with other people requires your brain to remain constantly alert to produce appropriate responses in spontaneously arising situations.

Solving brain-teasing problems can also help to refine your brainpower. Trying new approaches to problem solving can be a fruitful way of breaking out of well-trodden mental tracks, and stimulating new parts of your brain into action. Such techniques include lateral thinking and brainstorming.

Just as your body benefits from a physical workout, mental exercise helps to preserve and expand your brainpower. When you present your mind with novel information or activities to do, you are awakening new parts of your brain and strengthening underused neural communication lines.

Eating well is as important as mental exercise in maintaining brainpower. The whole range of nutrients your brain requires can best be secured by eating a healthy, balanced diet that includes a wide range of fresh fruit and vegetables, whole-grain products, fish, eggs, poultry, and low-fat dairy products, and is low in refined starches, sugar, and animal fats.

How perceptive are you?

Everyone knows people who, although evidently intelligent, appear to be slightly out of touch: they take no interest in what motivates other people, and have little empathy for what others may be feeling. What these people lack is Interpersonal Intelligence (II). Conventional accounts of intelligence, which concentrate heavily on a grasp of the world of ideas, seldom pay much attention to interpersonal skills. Yet people who possess above-average II are often natural leaders, arbitrators, judges, doctors, and teachers. Such people tend to be intensely interested in, and curious about, those around them, and they are often highly skilled at interpreting the subtle signs that reveal someone's emotional state.

Some of the emotions that people feel are expressed in nonverbal ways through body language. In your own relationships with friends, family, and acquaintances, an understanding or body language may be of use in helping you side-step confrontation or put other people at ease. In business, such an understanding can guide you successfully in closing a deal or act as and early-warning device to alert you when it's time to back off. And when you are with people you want to impress, you can use your knowledge of nonverbal language to present yourself in the most acceptable way, encouraging others to be more receptive to you.

How creative are you?

One commonsense way to determine whether you could be a creative person is to think back to problems you have faced in the past, and remember the ways you solved them. People with a proven record of creativity tend to be independent and nonconforming, and they posses an internal motivation that does not depend on rewards from the outside world. They do not assume that the status quo exists for a good reason – they know there is always room for improvement.

To bring out your most creative ideas, be flexible and original in your thinking. Allow your mind freedom to explore even the most unlikely avenues – the best solutions can appear in the most unexpected ways. Do not automatically reject ideas that seem, at first sight, to be ridiculous. And don't be satisfied with the most obvious answer to a problem. There may be a more fruitful solution just around the corner.

Overcome your mental blocks

Every individual has a capacity for growth and development, both in terms of the ability to acquire new skills, and in the unique qualities of his or her personality. Why, then, do many people grow older feeling that they have never fulfilled themselves or explored their abilities fully?

The answer often lies in deep-rooted fears and negative states of mind. They are ruinous mental blocks; they close off avenues of personal development, and prevent people from making the most of their lives.

One serious mental block from which many people suffer in varying degrees is the fear of failure. Another negative frame of mind that can stand in the way of self-improvement is typified by a sort of habitual submissiveness, which leaves people helpless when dealing with others who may be more powerful, assured, or dominant.

Finally, there is the mental block created by negative thinking. If you expect negative things to happen to you, your expectations are likely to be fulfilled. By developing a more optimistic outlook, you can reverse the spiral and begin to take positive steps toward a better life.

To fulfil your potential, free your mind from the cage of negative thoughts and unacknowledged fears.

Daring to fail

No one likes failure, or the feelings of inadequacy and humiliation that often accompany it. But fear of failure can be much worse that failure itself, because it can stop you from taking steps to change your life for the better. Without taking risks and daring to fail, it is impossible to learn, change, or develop. Mindy you, your chances of achieving happiness and success may depend on your doing all of those things.

Finding a way out of fear

One unfortunate consequence of having a fear of failure is that you can become isolated from the people around you.

It can be tempting to believe that people who appear confident and successful are immune to fear of failure. In most cases, this is not true. They have simply learned to deal with both the fear and the possibility of failure.

Fighting fear of failure

- Adopt a 'can-do' attitude
- Alter your thoughts about failure
- Keep your sense of proportion
- Stop avoiding what scares you
- Use your imagination positively
- Learn to relax!

Asserting Yourself

Self-assertion is a firm insistence that others pay you the heed and respect to which you are entitled as a human being.

If you are too self-effacing and submissive, people will tend to overlook you; if you are too overbearing and aggressive, on the other hand, people will probably avoid you.

Because you do not stand up for yourself, you are more likely to become the scapegoat for anything that goes wrong. People may take unfair advantage of you by borrowing money or asking favours, confident that you won't have the gumption to refuse or even ask that the debts be repaid. In extreme cases, your compliance may make you the victim of bullying.

What is appropriate assertiveness?

You have achieved the right degree of assertiveness when you are able to stand up for your rights, and make your thoughts and feelings clear to others. You must be prepared to refuse to do things that you don't want to do, and say 'no'. Some individuals adopt an aggressive and bullying manner to get their message across. But you are more likely to have success if you develop more controlled ways of asserting yourself. The majority of people who have difficulty in asserting themselves effectively do so, because they lack confidence and communication skills, not because they are unsuited by temperament.

How to practice self-assertion

Self-assertion often involves expressing what you want contrary to the wishes of other people. It is important to be clear in your mind about what you want to say. When you are rehearsing these scenarios, remember to utter your responses in a voice that is clear and self-confident. Make sure that your posture communicates determination, rather than a submissive disposition. Stand erect and look your imagined person directly in the eye.

Some people make self-assertion exercises more fun by practicing role-playing. Remember to think through beforehand everything you want to say. Take your time and make sure you are saying what you intended.

Assertive behaviour becomes easier as you develop confidence, so you need to think positively and develop your self-esteem. People will treat you differently, and they will show you the respect due to a more forceful individual.

How to get that raise:

- Practice your self-presentation
- Prepare yourself to negotiate
- Get ready to reply to a refusal
- Start well, and get the answer in writing

Learning to think positively

To develop positive thinking, begin with specific situations. If you have a challenging task to face, start by objectively identifying positive aspects of the task, and develop an upbeat attitude on this basis. You feel apprehensive and are worried about making a fool of yourself at a task that has been assigned to you. But before you start to have an anxiety attack, and decide you can't possibly do it, sit down and look at the situation objectively. There is certainly a number of reasons why you've been given this assignment, and there is really nothing to be afraid of, if you know the facts back-to-front. All that is needed is adequate preparation and a realistic belief in yourself.

Habitual negative thinking reduces your self-confidence and your ability to cope well with challenging situations; it may lead you to accept failure and defeat with resignation. All this often results in less and less success, which in turn causes more negative thinking. You create a downward spiral as your thoughts become self-fulfilling prophecies.

Do you have a healthy self-image? Or do you see yourself as a failure – an uninteresting or insignificant person? Your self-image reflects how you expect others to see you. To develop a strong and healthy self-image, make a comprehensive list of your attributes, your achievements, and your assets, and then take time to acknowledge and appreciate them. The effect may be quite dramatic.

Having a positive attitude does not always guarantee success. But even when the outcome of a situation is less than you might have hoped for, you will be able to deal with the outcome in a productive way.

Thinking positively means believing that success is a real possibility, giving yourself the best chance in every setting, and turning all experiences into valuable occasions for learning.

Quiet your mind

Emotional suffering and mental anguish are not necessary. Chronic emotional suffering is not our natural state. We're just emerging into a period of history when we can identify why we're continually torturing ourselves with unwanted emotions; blow the whistle on the root cause of our inner torment, confusion, and agitation; and then act to shift into more enjoyable, fulfilling realms of consciousness.

We assume that we function best, and enjoy life to the fullest, when we're habitually engaged in nonstop mental reflections, worries, plotting and judgments. In contrast, only through regularly quieting the entire flow of thoughts, images, memories, and reflections that fill our minds can we regain intimate and fulfilling contact with sensory, intuitive, and heart-felt experiences that emerge when we shift into direct encounter with the world around us.

We must choose between being absorbed in deductive verbal reasoning (a past-future function of the mind) and direct experience of the world (a present-moment function of the mind), because it's very difficult to do both at the same time. We do possess the inherent power to control the context of our thoughts and quiet chronic thought-flows altogether whenever we choose. A certain amount of mental problem solving and cognitive reflection is essential to human life, and can actually be quite fun.

Regularly entertaining uplifting thoughts, give philosophical meaning to our existence, and encourage positive feelings can be a great help in raising our spirits and spreading joy around us. However, all too often our habitual thought-flow carries a negative rather than a positive emotional edge, generated by old fear-based attitudes, assumptions, and beliefs that no longer correctly reflect our present reality. Such thoughts from outdated or distorted beliefs provoke anxious, aggressive, and depressive emotions – which in turn make us suffer.

Our emotions don't emerge suddenly out of nowhere. Just the opposite, they are almost always being stimulated by habitual thoughts and related images we keep running through our minds, often at a mostly subliminal level of awareness.

People suffering from chronic negative emotions such as anxiety and depression, anger and confusion, are taught to identify the recurrent thought flows that stimulate these negative emotions, and to replace these negative thoughts and beliefs with more positive and realistic ones. These new thoughts in turn stimulate positive emotions, encouraging an expanding sense of inner confidence and well-being. Self-applied cognitive therapy programmes can be of lasting benefit in the treatment of non-acute anxiety and depressive conditions.

When we focus our attention on just one bodily sensation, thoughts usually continue flowing through our mind. When we learn the simple mental process of fully focusing on two or more distinct bodily sensations at the same time (breathing and heartbeat) (sight and sound), all thoughts cease flowing through the mind. From subjective psychological studies to all meditative traditions, purposeful refocusing of one's mental attention in particular ways can directly and predictably quiet the flow of thoughts through the mind.

Emotional healing

From a therapeutic point of view, emotional healing requires an integration of feelings from the heart with ideas and thoughts from the cognitive centre of the brain.

By learning to live more deeply in the here and now, you can reduce physical stress and return your body to its natural healthy state, also getting revitalised in the process.

In mystic terminology, spirit isn't a phenomenon of our personal memory banks or our imaginations of a projected future. Spirit flows in through our hearts only when we are 'here' in the present moment. We tune into spiritual guidance not while we're busy 'talking to' God; but rather, when we're quiet and receptive in our minds.

It is very difficult, or even impossible, to think deductively while also focusing on two or more sensory inputs – the perceptual activity, by and large, short-circuits the thinking process.

The capacity of the logical thinking mind, the seat of the ego, to assume a certain amount of control over our lives can be very helpful – when regularly moderated and balanced by our intuitive, experiential, and spiritual dimensions. But all too often the deductive mind tends to become a 'control freak' that rules rigidly by pre-conceived fear-based expectations and beliefs – leaving little or no room for spontaneity and playful action motivated by the heart and soul. Our thoughts almost always stimulate emotional responses in our bodies, and when emotions are fear-based, our emotions are going to be no fun at all.

The memory-based thoughts, expectations, and assumptions, of left-brain thought-flows, deductive thoughts, are primarily responsible for stimulating anxiety, shame, anger and depression. Our right-brain is associated with 'thoughtless' feelings of compassion, joy, pleasure, well-being, and bliss.

When you quiet your habitual chattering ego thoughts, and tune your attention into heart-felt sensory experience, and then open up to an integrative experience of "everything at once", thoughts often do indeed begin to flow again. But here's the difference – these new thought-flows, emerging directly out of the here and now, and coming into being while you're deeply in touch with your heart and soul, will be of an entirely different quality than those that emerge semiautomatically from your conditioned past. These new thoughts will come into being without anxiety or other negative emotions polluting them, as a result of an integration of your intuitive and higher deductive capabilities. In essence, this is what insight is all about – this is how we suddenly find ourselves thinking inspired thoughts. We've quieted the chronic thoughts of our deductive mind, we've entered into a higher state of consciousness where spirit or higher wisdom can impact our personal lives – and in this expansive state of mind, we experience a spontaneous flow of thoughts inspired by our perception of the whole at once.

Spiritual masters have said very clearly in their own way, "Judge not, or you will be judged." This statement is one of the most insightful psychological observations about how the human mind works. If you go around continually judging everything you encounter, you're naturally going to end up totally caught up in judgment mode, and thus shut out from the more spiritual, heart-centred realms of a truly fulfilling life.

While our minds are busy judging a situation, we're mostly lost to the present moment, as we compare the present situation with all associated experiences in the past, and judge the newness of the present moment based not on the reality of the here and now, but rather on associations from the past.

Meanwhile, while we're busy in our minds comparing and contrasting, and also creating imaginary projections into the future about what might transpire, we've mostly lost our direct participation in the present moment.

Consider this. When you pause and look at a magnificent sunset, you're often overwhelmed by the beauty before you. You have a moment epiphany in which you transcend your ego boundaries and merge with the universe of which you are an integral part. But then what happens? Your thinking mind cuts into gear again, your inner voice starts doing its predictable commentary on the beauty of the sunset – you're back inside your own ego skin once again, "thinking about" the sunset rather than experiencing it directly beyond the bounds of cognitive comment.

The Power of Acceptance

When we're busy judging, our mind is creating inner dissonance by its insistence on evaluating if something should be different than it is right here, right now. As soon as we say, "I accept this just as it is", "I accept myself just the way I am", we open our hearts and embrace the world and ourselves.

As we accept our present reality without judgment, and let our love flow unconditionally into the situation, in effect we surrender all the attitudes that keep us distant and detached from the situation and thus become more lovingly involved with that situation. We become active participants, rather than judgmental observers. And by entering into such intimate participation in the unfolding present moments, our own loving presence, released from its judgmental inhibitions, begins to very actively influence the situation – so that, in fact, natural positive change is encouraged through our very presence.

By having our minds free to regularly tap our deeper spiritual wisdom and guidance regarding the situation, we will know directly from our intuitive depths when and how to act. Through the very act of accepting the world as it is, we become a powerful agent of positive change in the world.

We assume that acceptance leads to passivity. But loving acceptance leads to an active engagement that spreads our love and manifests our wisdom, and thus encourages rapid evolution of a situation. And throughout, love – not fear-based judgment – will be the motivating power.

Observing your own self

Through the simple act of looking with acceptance and love at your own judgmental habits (a very challenging mental operation), you will discover that you can initiate spontaneous positive change with those mental habits.

It seems almost impossible to improve your mind's judgmental habits towards others, unless you first learn to accept yourself as perfectly okay, just as you are. Self-help doesn't work without the presence of self-love. Then and only then, does spontaneous inner healing and deep personal growth occur.

By creatively employing our basic "animal response" to fear in new ways, we can generate positive change within our deepest conditional belief systems – by doing absolutely nothing at all except lovingly observing our own minds in action, without engaging in judgment of any kind.

It is key learning how to enter into a state of consciousness where you can observe your thoughts, without being totally consumed in or identified with them. This is what we practice with the basic breath, heart, whole-body meditation; the instant self-correction process we seek is activated only when we've shifted free of our usual past-fixated mode of thinking. Take time each day to observe your inner habits of mind clearly so as to perceive instantly the truth of the situation and evoke the proper inner response. The aim is to employ the self-correction power of your whole consciousness.

We all tend to make snap judgments; because of past conditioning of our amygdale, our conscious thoughts about a situation or person become negatively coloured even before we move through a realistic analysis of the situation. We almost instantly project a stereotype based on past experience onto the present moment.

We've all lived extremely full lives, and in the process had a great many experiences that left a lasting impression on us. The older we get, unless we consciously reverse the process, the more we tend to see the present moment as a function of the past rather than as something bright and new – and often unexpected.

The Forgiveness Factor

Rapid emotional healing occurs when the person lets go of beliefs about blame. When we stop blaming someone, we are performing the basic act of forgiveness. After learning how to forgive, rather than blame, you are less attached to bad feelings, and more likely to forgive in the future. Those who learn how to let go of blame, and accept reality without judgment, also usually experience a detectable reduction in stress, anger, and psychosomatic symptoms.

Forgiveness is often thought of as a somewhat mystic religious process, but we can apply the power of forgiveness within the psychological framework, by realizing that blame is based not on what someone else does or does not do in relation to us, but on what we choose to believe has happened to us as a result of what that person has done. In other words, forgiveness is simply the cognitive act of letting go of a judgmental belief that is not serving us.

Don't fight reality

In Buddhism it's said that our suffering is a direct expression of our distance from the truth. When we fully accept the reality of the past and the present moment, emotional suffering is reduced to a minimum. We deny what is true, and generate all sorts of negative emotions in the process. If we want to reduce our own inner suffering, and maximize enjoyment and peace in the present moment, we do best by accepting reality just as we find it, rather than resisting it just because it doesn't fit one of our beliefs or assumptions about how things should be. By denying the truth with judgmental thoughts, you shut yourself off from participation in life. By accepting reality just as it is, you become a transformative agent in that reality. You can't change the present moment. But reality is constantly evolving, and you can participate in that evolution.

Angry thoughts

We get angry mostly because of judgments we make (thoughts) that place blame and guilt on other people for doing things we don't think they should have. Is it true that they really did something they shouldn't have done? Are they really responsible for our hurt feelings? Do we have any right to project our beliefs or right and wrong into their lives, and throw blame upon their heads? Do we gain anything by fighting against the reality of what has happened?

Unless anger is provoked by a direct present-moment action on the part of the other person, anger is almost always a response to thoughts we're running through our minds, in which we're judging a person (or situation) as having unfairly caused us damage or upset in the past, or for planning to cause us damage in the future. Even though it's our own thoughts that are provoking our negative emotions, we blame the other person for causing us to be emotionally hurt or upset.

Now, consider the reality of the impact of anger upon our system. Unless we need to charge our bodies with aggressive power and then act physically to fight or run away, the charge of anger in our bodies is never going to serve us. This is almost always detrimental to our health and well-being. These thoughts are counterproductive in our lives. How can we act to quiet thoughts full of anger, blame and guilt projection?

Most angry thoughts and feelings can be defused quiet readily, once we learn to question whether the underlying assumption of belief that provoked our anger is valid. We can deactivate the entire anger-blame syndrome. This is the shortest route to forgiving and moving on.

Nothing good or bad

Shakespeare said: 'There's nothing good nor bad, but thinking makes it so'.

All religions, cultures, and social groups try to control the behaviour of their members by creating lists of rules of what is accepted and what is not accepted. Often these rules are given the weight of a religious dictum, and the moral play is acted out generation after generation. From the time we are very young, most of us are subjected to a barrage of verbal statements and beliefs which we accept, not on the basis of experience or even rational wisdom, but simply because we've been programmed to believe they're true – and we're afraid of what might happen to us if we even question them.

The key issue here is whether you trust your higher mental functions (the integrative intuitive perception of a quiet peaceful mind) to guide you so that you can set yourself free in the present moment, to act spontaneously as your heart and soul so move you.

Negative Core Beliefs

A great many of us go around constantly blaming other people for all our problems. An equal number go around blaming themselves for being no good, for being guilty, for being wrong… for being somehow unacceptable.

There are two core beliefs: the belief and feeling of being helpless; and the belief and feeling of being unlovable or unworthy.

These core beliefs are usually developed early in life, and often become submerged and even inactive unless extreme life situations are confronted. But such primal cognitive substrata will continue to subtly influence the general quality and content of the thoughts and resultant emotions a person manifests in life, until openly confronted and reconsidered.

For instance, when someone is blaming others for their problems, they're almost always actually feeling helpless and weak deep down, unable to fight for their own rights. They often have the habit of holding themselves chronically caught up in anger, to help bolster their underlying sense of being weak and helpless. Being helpless makes us feel frightened, and anger is a way of trying to overcome the feeling of being helpless.

A great many people suffer tremendously and chronically from depression and guilt, and furthermore sabotage opportunities for establishing loving relationships, because early in life they developed a core belief that they're somehow hopelessly unlovable.

Apply the basic de-believing process to whatever belief we find. Get to know yourself – you'll begin to have realizations that will transform your beliefs for the better. You don't have to replace old beliefs with new beliefs; you have the freedom of living your life more and more free of the domination of beliefs in general, by spending more time in spontaneous interaction with the world in the present moment.

When you are asked who you are, or when you ask yourself that question, instead of looking to your memory banks, instead of looking to your beliefs, look instead directly to the heart of your feeling of being alive right now, in this present moment. Who you are is to be found in how you spontaneously respond to the present moment.

Breaking free from worries

One particular aspect of fear is called anxiety, where the thinking mind fixates on possible problems and provokes anxiety with worrisome thoughts, regularly disturbing our peace of mind. People have an abject assumption of radical danger around every business curve. If fact, people realize that their father had held the same fear, and probably his grandfather as well. Their underlying childhood or inherited fear of losing everything, and dying destitute if they don't constantly worry and fight about business, is not a valid fear.

A great many physiological studies on stress have demonstrated that maintaining a chronic fearful state of mind and body (worry, being angry or aggressive, holding a constant state of readiness to fight or escape) does not serve anyone well. Chronic stress caused by too much worrying generates mental and physical fatigue, confusion, impatience, difficulty in all aspects of communication and relating. Worrying gets us nowhere fast.

De-beliefing

Make yourself comfortable… tune into your breathing… your heart… your whole body, here in this present moment… and now let your mind go back to an experience you had, where you felt afraid or threatened, in a particular situation that didn't really call for a fear reaction – where you were in no way threatened or harmed.

Remember the situation clearly… what you're doing, what you're seeing, what you're hearing around you… and because you know that you're not going to be hurt during the experience, instead of feeling fear in the situation, allow yourself to relax and feel safe and happy throughout the experience…

After you've relived the experience without feeling so much fear or no fear at all, say to yourself, 'I'm not afraid of having that experience; I enjoy the experience.'

Throughout the course of the day, turn your mind toward the experience or situation associated with fear, and remember your experience of being in the situation, and having nothing bad happen to you at all. In this way, actively decondition your mind from associating the situation with danger.

Replace old assumptions no longer valid with more realistic assumptions. Regularly vocalize and imagine your new assumptions, so that the amygdale hears the new information, and forms new paradigms to that situation. 'I don't have to be so afraid when I'm in a group situation like this. I'm mature and can take care of myself. There's nothing dangerous here, and I'm not afraid anymore'. 'The world's not going to end if I lose this job. I'm competent, I work hard, and I can always get another job'.

Self-judge not

Your attitude toward yourself, your entirely self-image, is purely a product of your past, not your present. You can't change the past, no matter how much you think about it and agonize over it and condemn it and wish you'd done otherwisc. The only thing you can do to free yourself from negative self-judgments based on the past is to just let go of it all, and focus on the present moment. When you are living in the present moment, how you feel right now determines who you are, not what you felt or did or had done to you in the past.

Giving and receiving

Human beings do 'touch' each other directly when they focus their attention on each other. The issue of direct transpersonal communication is of course not a new one. Throughout history, many of our wisest scholars and scientists have openly claimed that they could sense the presence of an invisible yet almost palpable power within their own minds. Isaac Newton, the patriarch of classic Western science; Francis Bacon, father of the experimental method, highly interested in studying such 'mind over matter' phenomena as telepathic dreams, psychic healing, transmission of spirits, and the power of the mind on the casting of dice; in contemporary physics, Max Planck, Neils Bohr, Albert Einstein, Werner Heisenberg, Erwin Schroedinger, and David Bohm. They have all written about the still-mysterious influence of consciousness on external matter and events.

After years of exploring 'consciousness/environment interaction' phenomenon, it has been concluded that there exists no distinct boundary between mind and matter at the wave-particle level of reality. Consciousness is allowed to permeate outward into its surrounding environment. Individual human consciousness does impact its environment, and emotional love is an active ingredient. The thoughts we think are not only influencing our own inner realms, they're also impacting the people around us.

When we broadcast fearful or judgmental thoughts, these thoughts are being received by other human beings, regardless of distance and time. So every time we slip into fear-based thoughts, we're broadcasting fear throughout the world. At this level, our business gets broadcast into everyone else's business.

Conversely, when we silence such fear-inducing thoughts, and tune into the natural peace and love within our hearts, we radiate this love demonstrably out to the world. This is perhaps the scientific explanation of how people still feel the love of Buddha or Mohammed or Jesus strongly in their hearts, even many centuries after their physical presence has left the earth.

Face-to-Face Contact Line

When we have our focus on the past, on memories and thoughts emerging from those memories, our hearts are simply puppets generating whatever emotions are associated with our past experiences. No learning is taking place, no healing is taking place, when we're just replaying memories and emotions from the past. However, we do have the freedom to manage our minds, the power to shift to the present moment. Let's say you meet someone new and are face-to-face with this person in the present moment. This person is unique, and if you stay in the present moment with them, and allow your perceptions and your heart feelings in the present moment to be dominant, you're going to have a unique encounter with this person, and develop a unique relationship based on the experiences that come to you in the present moment. Your heart is going to be able to respond directly to this person's heart as an experience, through all the sense inputs you're receiving of this person, and also through the more subtle communications where your minds and your hearts are interacting directly. You're going to interact. You're going to feel each other's presence directly, and meet, heart to heart. Something is going to happen between you, and this happening will continue to develop, moment to moment, as long as you remain focused on your present moment experience of each other, rather than on the memories that are already beginning to accumulate.

In the present moment, when we listen to what our hearts are telling us about what we're experiencing, we gain direct insight and wisdom into the deeper reality before us. Leading with the heart is our very best system for directly knowing the truth about the situation. This doesn't mean that we've shut down the rest of the brain. It means that we've integrated the entire brain into one intuitive whole; this is how we can be thoughtless, and totally lucid. This is how we can move through the power of love in the world and fear no harm – because love is not blind, love is the permeating creative force of the universe itself.

The power of attention

Begin focusing on good feelings that you have experienced in your heart, when you were in a loving mood, and feeling well-loved. Regularly focus your attention on memories that support your capacity to love and be loved. Shift out of the past, tune into whatever feelings you find in the present moment.

This special session is designed to be experienced perhaps once a week, for the rest of your life. We are continually in the process of dealing with old emotional wounds that have been rejected and buried earlier in our lives (usually from childhood), and are now finally rising to the surface to be accepted, experienced, and let go of. This is how we stay healthy emotionally – through regularly looking, accepting, releasing, and healing whatever emotional pleasure we might find within us.

Solitude

The essential challenge in all our lives is to master the fine art of developing a healthy, fulfilling relationship with ourselves. Why do so many of us fear solitude, and do everything we can to avoid being alone with ourselves without constant distraction? Because with our prevailing negative attitudes about our own selves, we're afraid to come face-to-face with aspects of our own selves that we reject, that we're afraid of, that we fear will make us suffer or react with self-loathing.

Escaping loneliness

Very often, we run away from the vacancy inside our own hearts, and try to immerse ourselves in social situations and relationships so that we feel loved, even if we don't love ourselves. This is a primary escape route for people who are lonely – they keep themselves constantly active at work, in social and church groups, in sports and family affairs. But they never quite get away from their sense of isolation from their own souls.

A great many people also try to escape their loneliness by becoming supergivers to the rest of the world. They are continually giving caring attention to those around them. They exert great effort to serve humankind, to seek and find love wherever they can. Many people also run from one love affair to the next, determined that they will someday find someone who will miraculously through the power of love, heal their hearts, make them feel whole inside, and take away the chronic ache of loneliness from their lives. It never works. When we don't love ourselves, and accept ourselves, how will anyone else be able to like us? We've made ourselves basically unlovable, and then complain about being lonely and no one loving us.

The first step in successfully moving out into the world to claim your fair portion of the universal wealth is to make sure that before you have your first encounter of the day, you have consciously assumed control of your own mind, and ensure that you're in optimum inner condition for a successful encounter.

Begin to discipline yourself each and every morning by setting aside five minutes before heading out into the world, to clarify in your mind the priorities that you're going to hold to throughout the day.

With every single person you encounter in the next twenty-four hours, notice if you are more successful with that person if you are afraid and therefore aggressive, judgmental, and defensive toward the person – or if you let go of your fears, open up, and relate in love and acceptance.

The executive who walks into a meeting radiating compassion, harmony, and a readiness to cooperate with the other people in the room, is going to succeed far beyond the executive who walks into the room hostile, defensive, ready to do battle to defeat everyone he perceives as his enemy.

When you find yourself feeling any negative emotion in your heart, catch the thought or memory or assumption that is generating the emotion. When you're in action at work and find that you're feeling hostile toward someone, or afraid in their presence, or judgmental about them – all you have to do is take a deep breath, shift from judgmental to heartfelt feelings and say silently: 'I'm sorry I was judging you. I accept you just as you are and open my heart to you'.

Work in the present moment

The primary activity at work isn't problem solving, in which constant thinking is primary. The dominant activity in most business involves learning more about a situation, communicating about a situation, and brainstorming intuitively to gain a broader understanding of a situation. The company that succeeds best will naturally be the company that is regularly tuning in to what's happening in the present moment so as to gain maximum information, before doing the cognitive process of transforming the perceptual data into a meaningful concept. I strongly recommend that in every workplace, everyone be encouraged, to pause for a few minutes from their fixation upon their particular item of concern, to relax and take a few deep breaths, shift into whole-body heart-centred attention in the present moment, and take in the whole of the situation.

Business

Business is a process whereby a group of individuals agree to put their attention together during a certain period of time, to accomplish a shared goal. When individuals come together to work as a team, two things need to happen: They all need to maintain the greater vision of the goal, so that they indeed work toward the same accomplishment, and each person needs to do what he or she does by fixating on a particular aspect of the project.

A principal difficulty is that as time goes by, individual team players tend to get so caught up in their special fixation on a part of the goal, that they progressively lose touch with the greater vision. Another main difficulty is the erosion of performance and team spirit caused by fear-based thoughts and resultant emotions that begin to dominate the atmosphere of the workplace. Over time, hundreds of relatively small negative encounters have gone unaddressed, and worried thoughts have spread like a cancer throughout the minds of the workers – to where hearts have shut, minds are a confusion of hostile and upset thoughts, bodies are tense and unhealthy, and love is pretty much nonexistent.

In most cases, the solution to such a negative work atmosphere doesn't have to be firing everybody or putting everybody into therapy. The solution can be a gentle regular five-minute break, during which everyone is simply guided into feeling better in their bodies, quieting their thoughts altogether for long enough, and encouraging everyone to focus on the shared vision of the company to work together in harmony, to accomplish a shared goal. A business is only as good as its employees. An employer doesn't have a right to impose any individual mind-management or cognitive-therapy training, or indeed any hourly or daily group training program, on employees. It's perfectly okay to provide a regular five-minute breather that allows and even guides employees into a more present-moment, enjoyable state of mind and body, but a line must be drawn at work between simple relaxation breaks and concerted mind-management training. Personal growth is a personal matter, not a company matter. It's extremely important that employees have total freedom to decide whether they want to participate in such programs, and not be penalized in any way if they choose not to.

The essence of Reich's therapy techniques is to have clients lie down on their back on the floor and just do nothing – except breathe deeply through the mouth. What Reich discovered was that the human organism, when given half a chance, would naturally begin to heal itself through the spontaneous release of emotions and the flood of memories and thoughts, beliefs and movements that accompanied the release of the pent-up emotions.

Reich insisted that we cannot live a full life, until we learn to regularly shift out of the thinking manipulating mind, into functions of the mind where the whole being is choosing what to do, each and every new moment of the day. Passion is what happens when we surrender mental control of our organism, and trust in our deeper self to choose the appropriate action. When thoughts stop, the body still knows what to do – and does it with perfection and pleasure unknown to the thinking mind. Sexual passion does not emerge from the activity of the thinking mind. In fact, as soon as we start thinking, passion begins to retreat from the scene. Passion is a feeling in the heart and the genitals; it is a function of perceptions and feelings that probably predate our thinking minds by many thousands of years. More specifically, sexual passion happens as an integrated phenomenon when our full range of senses perceive a situation where we are free to let go of all fears and problems, as we shift into pure sensation and emotion. Most of us hunger for this primal release on a regular basis, because it makes us feel so good as it quiets our usual worries and concerns, blows off pent-up emotions, opens our hearts – and at least momentarily shifts us into states of consciousness where we feel one with our sexual partner and with the entire universe.

Your childhood upbringing strongly conditioned you with beliefs about your sexuality, and how you should behave sexually. However, most of such childhood programming related to sex ends up hindering true sexual union, rather than augmenting it.

If you want to have fulfilling sexual intercourse, you cannot close your heart to experiencing your own spiritual core of being. Making love means intimately experiencing the creator – you're plugging directly into the ultimate creative power of the universe when you make love.

A Good Night's Sleep

Getting a good night's sleep is a universal challenge that the majority of us struggle with on a nightly basis, often unsuccessfully. Doctors and psychologists have identified a variety of possible reasons for sleeplessness. We spend nearly a third of our lives sleeping, and we suffer greatly when regular sleep eludes us. Sleeplessness is usually caused by all the various upsetting thoughts running through our minds as we get into bed. A bit of mental detective work, along with some de-beliefing, emotional healing, and heart opening, should provide you with the help you need to improve your sleep experience considerably. Sleep disorders, when untreated over time, can seriously disrupt your entire life. Sleeping pills are not the answer. Most sleeping pills are dangerous substances and have been overused... insomnia is not an illness for which a sleeping pill is a cure. Most often the cause will be behavioural or psychiatric (anxiety or depression) or medical.

Worries

Going to bed with your mind full of worried thoughts is definitely the primary cause of insomnia. When you're anxious, your nervous system is on alert because you're feeling threatened. And when you're in danger, it's not a good idea to doze off. You must deal with your worries and quiet them if you want to sleep well.

Excitement

Often we can't fall asleep because we're too excited about something happening the next day, or sometime in the future.

Environmental stress

A dog barking, a neighbour playing unsoothing music, sounds at night. The secret to dealing with environmental stressors is to examine the assumptions that underlie your thinking ('I can't ever get to sleep when dogs are barking'). Let go of those beliefs – and then shift your focus of attention away from listening to two or more sensory inputs that aren't related to sound: your breathing, your heart.

Irritation and pain

Both temporary and chronic insomnia are sometimes caused by physical pain. A plugged-up nose, a sinus headache, skin allergies, a painful bruise or cut. Shifting your attention to your breathing and heartbeat can work wonders. Let go of thoughts such as, 'I can never get to sleep when I have a cold'.

Stress from work

A great many of us carry our business concerns home with us; put a halt to business problem solving when you go to bed.

Caffeinated drinks

Change your choice of drinks: coffee, cans of cola, chai tea, all have caffeine. You will benefit greatly from doing ten to fifteen minutes of exercises, walking, dancing, or any other physical activity that will blow off the energetic charge and let you relax.

Everyday drugs

Many prescription medications such as mood elevators and diet pills will also keep you awake; they won't let the nervous system relax and sink into a good sleep.

Rejection and abandonment

Many people can't fall asleep because they're feeling rejected or abandoned by a lover, a parent, a group, their workplace, or some other organization. Such separation anxiety is a primal fear. You'll need to reassure yourself that you can survive, you can take care of yourself, and you can love yourself and find a new love.

Depression

When we feel that we're not good and everything's hopeless in life, then getting to sleep is very difficult – because the underlying beliefs generating our depressed thoughts and feelings are telling us that we can't survive, we can't carry on – and this basic assumption will keep us awake for fear of actually ceasing to exist at all. Depressive thoughts do have a way or rising to the fore when we are ready to go to bed and are done with the day. For one week or so, write down the thoughts you think when you're in bed, really get to know the underlying thoughts that are polluting your mind and keeping you awake. Then apply the techniques you already know to transcend the beliefs that are making you suffer.

Look to the feelings inside you, see what thoughts emerge, let those thoughts be there for a short time, and then say to yourself, 'I don't want to have those thoughts anymore', 'Everything's okay', 'I let it all go'.

Fear of death

The ultimate separation anxiety we face is of course our own demise, where our ego will probably dissolve as our deeper spiritual identity and consciousness move through the utter mystery of what comes after physical death. The solution lies in observing exactly what thoughts we're thinking about death, and the underlying assumptions we believe in concerning death. Worrying about death is clearly a future-projection act of the mind. Bring yourself into the perceptual-intuitive realms of consciousness in the present moment, to quiet your worries and let go of the future fear.

Smart Moves

Consider doing just five minutes of movement before bed if sleeplessness is a regular problem for you. As human beings we are clearly defined by our need and desire for regular movement. We know we're alive by the movement of our breathing and hearts. To live is to move. Yet most of us don't move too much during the day. If insomnia is a problem for you, I strongly recommend getting out and walking for half an hour to an hour a day. Before going to bed, you might want to put on some slow music that you love, and move to the music to release tensions in your body. Making sure the music is relaxing and slow, and that you give yourself permission to enjoy yourself. Don't force yourself to do particular motions – free spontaneous movement of any kind will bring your body, your spirit, and your mind into rapid harmony, and ready you for deep relaxation and sleep.

Meditation

Many people find the best cure for insomnia is a regular evening meditation practice, where they sit quietly for half an hour or so, quiet their minds, still their emotions, and enter a state of inner peace and acceptance of life.

Pause and Experience

Even while reading these words, you can begin to expand your awareness in experiential directions by also becoming aware of the air flowing in and out your nose or mouth as you breathe… Don't do anything to change your breathing. Just experience your mind's attention beginning to expand to include not only ideas and symbols but also your own body here in the present moment… and as you continue reading these words, and feeling the sensation of the air rushing in and out of your nose or mouth, also begin to be aware of the sounds around you… and when you come to the end of this paragraph, see what unique experience comes to you as you close the book momentarily, and tune fully into your breathing experience… your whole body here in the present moment… the sounds… the colours…

After reading this paragraph, if you like, choose to put the book aside for a couple of minutes, close your eyes, and gently turn your mind toward the actual physical sensation of the air flowing in and out your nose as you breathe. At the same time, be aware of the movements in your chest and belly as you breathe… and at the same time, be aware of any sounds around you as you continue breathing… and notice how your mind has become more quiet…

You are presently engaged in reading this logical flow of symbols, clearly a left-brain deductive function of the mind. After reading this paragraph, see what experience comes to you that might be of a more intuitive or even spiritual nature, as you put the book aside and again tune into your breathing experience… and at the same time, your heart… the sounds all around you… what your eyes see as you look around the room… and as you experience from the inside out your brain shifting its functioning, be open to a new experience…

After reading through this paragraph, put the book aside and close your eyes, tune into your breathing… and imagine that someone you know quite well comes into the room, but doesn't see you… They sit down, turn on the television, or pick up a book to read. Notice what your mind does, what thoughts emerge, as you watch this person. Don't judge your own thoughts, just observe them in action…

Close your eyes, and again, think of someone you know – just whoever pops into mind. Observe what thoughts and images come to mind when you think about what upsets you about this person, what you'd like to see change or improve… Now see what happens in your mind, when you temporarily just let go of all your judgments about this person and accept them just as they are, in the open-hearted spirit of love…

Pause after reading, close your eyes, tune into your breathing… and let yourself think of a person or situation you've been angry at or worrying about recently. Observe the way in which you tend to assume responsibility for another person's business. And then see how you feel when you stop intruding into their personal world, and say to yourself, 'What they do is none of my business'.

Tune into your breathing... your heart... your whole-body presence here and now... and as you look to your own inner core, reflect upon whether you trust your deeper heartfelt feelings and intuitive insights, and perhaps spiritual awareness as well, to successfully guide you through your life, beyond the strictures of the right-and-wrong rules you were programmed with as a child. Are you to be trusted as a spontaneous human being?

Soul Food

There is a place within each of us that is the source of fearlessness, compassion, and integrity. It is this place that inspires us to reach out a hand of comfort to a friend in need, to intervene to prevent the infliction of pain upon another. It is this place that grieves at the pain in our world and rejoices in the happiness and love that is found. When we are vitally connected to our own hearts, we know that all living beings wish to be free from pain and to live in peace and freedom.

Compassion and love do not need grand gestures and dramatic expression. Our opportunities for love, forgiveness, and reverence are manifold. Each time we respond with love we create a world of peace and integrity. Every response is worthy, significant, each makes a difference.

There are moments when we encounter feelings of despair, doubt, and inadequacy. We may wonder how to bridge the apparently uncrossable gap between confusion and clarity, holding and opening, limitation and freedom. In all moments of darkness we need to remember the capacity to be aware, the power to be conscious, to be awake, and to transform. It is an immense power, enabling us to penetrate the veils of confusion that limits us, enabling us to connect with and use the inner resources of energy, focus, and love that lie dormant.

The present moment is the most profound and challenging teacher we will ever meet in our lives. It is a compassionate teacher, it extends to us no judgment, no censure, no measurement of success and failure. The present moment is a mirror, and in its reflection we learn how to see. In this mirror we see what contributes to the confusion and discord in our lives and what contributes to harmony and understanding, what it is that connects us and what it is that alienates us.

The clutter of our lives blinds us to the precious simplicity that surrounds us and is within us. Too often we become possessed and imprisoned by the chains of our own accumulations. We live in fear of their loss; we evolve complex strategies to protect ourselves from failure and deprivation. This burden inhibits our ability to walk with lightness of heart. The noise created through our own busyness deafens us to the wonder of silence.

The energy employed in the judging mind is sufficient to transform the world. It is an energy we need to rechannel. Forgiveness, tolerance, patience, and love bring us humility. They remind us that the person we see before us is simply ourselves in another form, someone who yearns for the same love, acceptance, and open-heartedness that we yearn for, is capable of suffering the same pain of rejection, judgment, and hatred that we are capable of suffering.

In making new beginnings and travelling new paths, we need to be acutely watchful of our insecurities and self-doubt. These feelings can lead us to settle for boundaries rather than to expand our horizons. If we fear aloneness and seek reassurance, sanction, and identity through belonging, we will be led to blind belief rather than wise faith. It is insecure faith that is then translated into bigoted faith. Foolishness is the offspring of this insecure faith, sentencing us to being perpetual followers, listening to others rather than to ourselves.

Wise faith opens us rather than narrows us. It encourages us to question, to explore, to enquire. It encourages us to discover our own answers and to trust in our own experience. Wise faith enables us to listen to and learn from the guidance and experience of others while knowing that the power of transformation lies within. The greatest faith is the faith that we have in ourselves to live as fully compassionate and loving human beings.

As it matures, true faith, combined with wisdom, brings with it great humour and delight, a perspective of love and awareness so great that it encompasses the pain, the absurdities, the ironies, and the complexities of humanity.

Modern culture would have us worship before the altar of the thinking mind, with its endless capacity to produce ideas, fantasies, and formulas. We are taught that the thinking mind is the possessor of all wisdom, and we dedicate much of our lives to the pursuit of knowledge and information. Seeing the world and ourselves through the filter of all the information we have accumulated, we can become imprisoned by the very ideas and images we have so ardently pursued. Often we think that we know ourselves, when what we know is only what we think about ourselves, and we can't see the mystery held within each changing moment.

What is an image, if not just a description of the world that is bound to the past? What is a belief, if not just an insecure faith that has found sanctuary in a system?

It is especially easy for the mind to get caught in or blinded by religious ideals, by images or beliefs about how things should be. There are so many authorities and opinions dispensing models and images of who we should become, and what we should aspire to, so many teachings about what is holy and what is not. All of the Scriptures and guidance we listen to can at best point to a possibility, to the presence of a great mystery, that is just here before us.

We might reflect on what religious or spiritual ideas we may be holding on to that keep us from seeing what is true, that keep us from seeing directly our authentic path, guides, and teachers. What is present now in our own lives that is truly our spiritual teaching and practice, in that it offers us the opportunity to deepen our understanding? What would our lives be like if we carried no burden of 'should'?

Cause and effect

We seem to live in a random universe composed of accidental and haphazard events and experiences. Our movements from heaven to hell, from the heights of elation to the depths of despair, appear intractable and unpredictable. We use words like luck, fate, destiny, and jinx, to make sense of the variety of experiences that seem to 'just happen' to us. Lost in either despair or exhilaration, we do not see the threads of cause and effect that weave the tapestry of our lives (karma).

Karma does not mean belief in reincarnation and past lives. Karma is simply this law of cause and effect. If you plant an apple seed, you don't get a mango tree. If we practice hatred or greed, it becomes our way and the world responds accordingly. If we practice awareness or loving-kindness, it becomes our way and the world responds accordingly.

Like an artist before an easel, we paint the landscape of our life with the colours of our thoughts, values, actions, and feelings. The quality of our life is flavoured by the quality of each feeling and gesture. We are heirs to the results of our actions, to the intentions we bring to every movement we initiate. We make ripples upon the ocean of the universe through our very presence.

We are no different from anyone else. There is not one mistake we have made that has not been made before by another, not one delight we have experienced that has not been felt before by another. We see ourselves in others, and they in us. How can we know what is good or bad, or what lessons we need? What matters is how we respond. What we create, how we act and respond, embodies itself not only in our lives but in the lives of our communities, our children, our world. How we hold the world in our eye and heart is what we and the world will become.

Understanding the implications of our presence in the universe encourages us to see the importance of being awake and aware in each moment in our lives. As a conscious participant in the creation of each moment, of the world we live in, we have the power to heal, to love, to care, and to make our compassion visible.

You can't stop the waves, but you can learn to surf. We cannot control or stop the changing circumstances in our lives, but we can learn to balance amid them and to bring balance to them. Learning that poise and balance is the greatest skill in spiritual life: knowing when energy and resolution is needed and when it is time to soften and surrender; knowing when we need greater faith or greater inquiry; knowing when to seek greater solitude and simplicity or a time for service, to make our care and love visible. There is no formula for this responsiveness. We must simply learn to listen with an open heart to what is ever in this moment, this day, this life.

Serenity is not some lofty peak we inhabit after transcending the world, but is in learning how to respond to the challenges of this very life with great love. Wisdom is not an attainment but a way of being, a way of responding in which we neither resist the challenges life brings us, nor are overwhelmed by them. It is a question of balance.

We are witnesses to an age of endless conflict and destruction. Our planet suffers, human relationships break down, and individuals live in alienation. The wealth of ideas and formulas that have been produced have yet to bring about any meaningful shift in this cycle of pain. The pain of our world will not be changed by yet more ideas. What is needed is a profound change in the human heart. Let us not respond to the pain that surrounds us with righteousness, pious formulas, or withdrawal; let us learn how to respond with love and integrity. Let us not allow our lives to become a record of all the things we wish we had done, might have done, or should have done.

How to make our lives an embodiment of wisdom and compassion is the greatest challenge spiritual seekers face. Our every thought, word, or action holds the possibility of being a living expression of clarity and love. It is not enough to be a possessor of wisdom. Ideas and memories do not hold liberating or healing power. Profound love, compassion, sensitivity, and awakening move us, yet it is easier to love a thousand people in our thoughts than to fully love one person in actuality. It is not difficult to extend boundless acceptance and compassion to those who do not actively challenge us. Only in the midst of our concrete relationships and day-to-day living can we actually express our wisdom and demonstrate compassion.

Every word we speak, every action we initiate creates a ripple in our connectedness with life. Understanding this connectedness brings a sacredness to each moment. There is no contact, no perception, no engagement that is inconsequential or insignificant. Each contact is an opportunity for deepening sensitivity and understanding.

When our interpretation about the universe is still, when we no longer locate ourselves in past or future or yearn to become someone or something, a profound silence is revealed. This silence embraces all time and place, all change. It is not the opposite of movement but is the essential background that holds and embraces all movement.

As we deepen in silence, we discover that all things inner and outer are connected in the fabric of our consciousness. All things – we, too –, arise for a time and then disappear back into emptiness. Our infancy and our youth feel like fleeting moments that have vanished, together with the dinosaurs, the pharaohs, the ice caps. Each day and each moment appears, and then strides offstage to make space for the next. When we are silent, we are astonished to see how life renews itself in form after form, moment after moment. All these changing moments and forms are bound together by an abiding silence.

Never before has there been an age when the spiritual richness of the centuries has been so accessible. But there is no standard map to enlightenment. The fundamental message of every great spiritual teacher is that we must learn to see through our own eyes and to travel this path ourselves. We ourselves must discover how to bring integrity, compassion, attention, into blossom. An authentic spiritual path is one in which we learn to deepen the joy, harmony, and clarity of each day. We will know the genuine path by our own experience, if we are transformed and liberated each day.

What do we wish to give back to this earth? How can we enhance the well-being of our world? In discovering a path that awakens us, we also discover tremendous gratitude. We have been cared for in so many ways, large and small. We have been supported, guided, and loved. There rests within the heart of wisdom a longing to give to, to support, and to care for the world that has nourished us. We may offer our gifts through silence or through action; it is the giving that enables us to fulfil our time here with as much love and compassion as possible.

Letting go into Our Freedom

Letting go is the essence of the spiritual life, the heart of the spiritual practice. Only when we are no longer full of opinions and expectations are we truly receptive. Only when we are no longer afraid of loss do we begin to open in a whole-hearted way to the world around us. In the discovery of aloneness is the discovery of what it means to be truly together with others. Letting go is an expression of compassion for ourselves and love for the universe we live in.

In travelling this path of inner transformation, we are encouraged to let go of preoccupations with the past, investment in the future, and clinging in the present. We are encouraged to renounce our images, expectations, fears, and guilt. We are taught that holding is the path to limitation, letting go the direct path to awakening. This letting go is what allows us to be fully present here, rather than occupied with what was or what we hope for.

Letting go is inevitably a process of letting go into greater and greater capacities of being, from infant to child, adolescent to adult. Letting go of our fears and habits allows a more spacious wisdom to emerge.

When we see clearly, we discover that we are never actually the owners, the possessors, of the things in our life. Our homes, the things we call mine, even our children are here with us only for a time. Even our bodies do not belong to us. They are gifts, which will change and eventually need to be released in their own way. We are asked to relate wisely to them and all things, not by holding and possessing but by loving.

Laws of Cognition and Exposure

There are two laws that govern your life. The first is what might be called the law of cognition: You are what you think. One's thoughts influence every aspect of one's being. Whether we are filled with confidence or fear depends on the kind of thoughts that habitually occupy our minds.

Cognitive psychology is built around the truth that the way you think is the single most determinative about you. The way you think creates your attitudes; the way you think shapes your emotions; the way you think governs your behaviour; the way you think deeply influences your immune system and vulnerability to illness. Everything about you flows out of the way you think. Over the long haul, good thinking – accurate perceptions, healthy emotions, wholesome desires, honourable intentions – cannot produce bad results; bad thinking cannot produce good results.

The second law might be called the law of exposure: Your mind will think most about what it is most exposed to. What repeatedly enters your mind occupies your mind, eventually shapes your mind, and will ultimately express itself in what you do and who you become. People are surprised that what their minds are constantly exposed to, attend to, and dwell on eventually comes out in how they feel and what they do.

It is amazing to me how often people think or live as if they could get away with violating the law of exposure. The events you attend, the material you read (or don't), the music you hear, the images you watch, the conversations you hold, the daydreams you entertain – all are shaping your mind, and, ultimately, your character and destiny.

The good news is that you can put these laws to work for you. If you really want to become a certain kind of person you must begin to think thoughts that will produce those characteristics. The power of such practices is not simply that they change the patterns of the mind, though that in itself has considerable power. The real significance of this way of life is that it opens you wide to spiritual reality and power that was in fact all around you all the time, like a radio antenna suddenly tuned in to the right frequency. There are undiscovered continents of spiritual living available to anyone who would diligently open themselves up to them.

You may feel that meditation is something only monks and mystics can do. Do you know how to worry? If you can worry, you can meditate. To meditate merely means to think about something over and over. Let it simmer in your mind. Reflect on it from different angles until it becomes part of you.

Approach what you find repulsive, help the ones you think you cannot help, and go to the places that scare you.

We can use difficult situations – poison – as fuel for waking up. Breathe it in, instead of trying to get rid of it. Often in our lives we panic. We feel heart palpitations and stomach rumblings, because we are arguing with someone, or because we had a beautiful plan, and it's not working out. How do we deal with those demons?

We can dissolve the sense of dualism between us and them, between this and that, between here and there, by moving toward what we find difficult and wish to push away. There is nothing to be embarrassed about. Meditate on what provokes resentment. Lean into the sharp points. The instruction is not to try to solve the problem, but instead make us up further rather than lull us into ignorance. We can use a difficult situation to encourage ourselves to take a leap, to step into that ambiguity.

Success

We all have to come to terms with our own talents and skills, and figure out what we can do with them. It is possible to become something. You can have all the dreams you want, but you need to put something towards those dreams to make them work. If you want to run a café you need to know what people eat, how to make it, how to draw up a budget, some money to put, freedom to work a lot, you need to like people, and be prepared not to make any real money for maybe a year. It is only when you have a firm idea of what you want to do that you can work towards it. You need to think about where you will live and how you will live. In the country? In a house? Are you going to sell your house? Are you going to rent one? What work what will you do?

You need to start somewhere and that means starting small. 'I thought that working for other people was wasting my skills. I was able to move onwards not by aiming for the top job, but by doing one thing at a time. I also stuck to a path. I didn't decide that after being a printer I wanted to manage a record shop. You can't go firing in all directions. You have to stick to the same area, so that you can take what you have learned with you.'

Being the leader only becomes your job because you have done all the other jobs. You have to earn it. Life is about taking steps that move you forwards. You don't have to worry about going forwards quickly. What matters is that you are moving and that you keep moving until you hit your limits.

Stop looking for approval from others. Just because you want to do something doesn't mean the rest of the world shares your delight. If you want to start something, you can't wait for everything to be in place. You have to start somewhere. It's a mixture of being prepared enough, but not putting it off until you think it's all perfect. Optimism is something you have to fight for every day. You will have days when you feel you have sunk a little, and then you will have others when you bounce back. If you have a plan and believe in it, you will ride this roller coaster and come out of it the right way at the end. In many ways your success depends on your ability to direct your emotions and feelings the right way.

Whether you are looking to start a self-improvement programme or get your finances in order, there is no perfect time. Business people who have had success don't wait for the perfect time to start something. If they wait too long, someone else will come along under their nose. So, what they do is jump in, and solve problems as they come up. It is very rare that the people, money, emotions, skills and even the planets come together exactly when you want them to. Sometimes you just have to go with what you have. Restrict the people you listen to. Ask people, 'What I want from you, is some idea of what you think my biggest obstacle will be, and how I might get over that'. Life is about learning to adapt and adopt as you progress. You have to see how you get on with people, or you will be forever looking.

All success lies out of your comfort zone. The need to climb over your own personal fence comes when you realise you are not getting what you need inside it. When you reach a place where you are more and more unhappy with your life, you have to get out of your comfort zone. If you keep doing what you've always done, then you'll keep getting what you've always got.

It's great that people are becoming more interested in what is going on around them and in helping others. It's great that more young people have ideals that go beyond making money. It's great that they are willing to go out on a limb to make things happen. What's worrying is misplaced ideals, where people haven't thought about how things will work in a practical way. Then they get upset when nobody listens to them. It's wonderful to have visions of something better for you, your family, your community or the world. But you need to have thought about how you can make them work in real life. For example, you can't be emotional when you want to make changes in society. You have to look at the facts and be very practical.

Even if you have the best idea in the world, people may not buy it. Think about J.K Rowling. You, like her, must put a lot of effort into selling your idea. Don't just think, 'But it's so good, why can't they see it?' People can't see it because they're not you, so what you have to do is show them, step by step, what you are seeing. The more you believe in your idea, the better you will be able to see it. It will show in your face and your body language. You will speak in a more confident voice and you will even walk tall. When you truly believe in what you are doing, you can convince people even when things are bad.

To get someone to believe in your dreams, your ideas or indeed in you, you need to make them feel that if they don't listen they might be missing out on something. Even if you have some questions that you haven't quite answered yourself – which you will – you have to sound like you have it worked out 100 per cent.

Don't take the hardest task first to prove how tough or commanding you are. Taking on the easier steps first doesn't make you a lesser person. Start by asking people the easy questions, the ones they can answer, and then things will be a lot smoother.

Problems never stop. If you start a business, they never do. But failing is a big part of the learning process that we must go through in order to advance ourselves in life. The challenge isn't in the process of failing or making a mistake. It's in how we behave and move on when we make mistakes. Many of the people who have done very well in our society have failed many more times than they have succeeded. The difference is that they kept at it until they found a way to make it work. 'Smart people learn from their mistakes, smarter people learn from other people's mistakes, and the smartest people learn from smart people's mistakes'. However, the big businesses that run our world do not accept failure. They will say things like, 'We expect our employees to perform to the highest standards', but what they mean is, 'We're watching you and don't you dare fail, or we'll replace you'.

There are people who are willing to risk it all and fail; if not, we would not have much greatness in the world. The more creative you are, the more errors you will make. The more failures you have, and the more quickly they happen, the quicker you will learn. Because each time you fail you move closer to success. Edison said that he did not failed 10,000 times to invent the light bulb, but that he discovered 10,000 ways not to invent the light bulb. He saw his failed attempts as chances to learn.

It can often be useful to compare yourself with someone who is doing the same thing as you. Someone you admire, or even someone you don't admire in the same field. You need to know what other people are doing right, and what they are not doing right.

Success increases your chances of having another success. 'I changed. I feel more respect for myself. I get more joy from what I do. It is less like hard work and more like a way of living. I have lost many of the worries that go with starting something that you don't know will work. I have a greater depth to my thinking. I have a greater control of my anger. I am a more useful man. I waste less time. And I meet people who are themselves more useful. Then there are my energy levels which have gone through the roof. The energy comes from the kind of direction and focus that comes with success. I am not wasting it on unproductive things. Money is a by-product of success. It is not the success itself.'

Doing what you enjoy and being happy with your choices are more important than just doing something for money. If you are happy and working hard at something that happens to be money-making, then chances are that you will do very well.

Everything you've done until now, good and bad, has not been wasting time, but has brought you to where you are now.

What are your skills? What are your dreams? How can you make them match?

You may have to water down or fine-tune a dream to match your skills.

Part of thinking is believing. You need to believe in yourself, no matter what others think of you. You have to fight for optimism every day.

Look at things with a cool eye and an even cooler head. It's very nice to have great ideas, but unless you can make them work in real life, they are not great ideas. And unless you can sell them to the people who need to believe in them, they're useless. Success is a series of small steps that add up. It's not about shouting or arm waving. It's about taking on the small things first, the things you can do easily so that you get something under your belt. When you have that, you will also have the confidence to take on more. The world owes you nothing, but it will give you something if you put in the effort.

Just the Thought of It…

Whether we realize it or not, we are thinking most of the time. If you are speaking or listening to someone, you are thinking. If you are reading the newspaper or watching television, you are thinking. When you recall memories from your past, you are thinking. When you are considering something in your future, you are thinking. When you are driving, you are thinking. When you are getting ready in the morning, you are thinking. The forces of attraction are still operating on our last thoughts as we fall asleep. (So, make your last thoughts before going to sleep good thoughts.)

The laws of attraction and thinking work as an ongoing process. You don't press pause, you don't press stop. It is forever in action, as your thoughts are.

Creation is always happening. Every time an individual has a thought, or a prolonged way of thinking, they're in the creation process. Something is going to manifest out of those thoughts.

What you are thinking now is creating your future life. You create your life with your thoughts. Because you are always thinking, you are always creating. What you think about the most or focus on the most, is what will appear as your life.

You create your life. Whatever you sow, you reap! Your thoughts are seeds, and the harvest you reap will depend on the seeds you plant.

If you are complaining, the law of attraction will powerfully bring into your life more situations for you to complain about. If you are listening to someone else complain and focusing on that, sympathising with them, agreeing with them, in that moment, you are attracting more situations to yourself to complain about. The law is simply reflecting and giving back to you exactly what you are focusing on with your thoughts. With this powerful knowledge, you can completely change every circumstance and event in your entire life, by changing the way you think.

If you can think about what you want in your mind, and make that your dominant thought, you will bring it into your life.

Thoughts become things. Say this over to yourself and let it seep into your consciousness and your awareness.

Thoughts are vibration in specific frequences. Thoughts are sending out that magnetic signal that is drawing the parallel back to you. The predominant thought or the mental attitude is the magnet, and the law is that like attracts like, consequently, the mental attitude will invariably attract such conditions as correspond to its nature.

Thoughts are magnetic, and thoughts have a frequency. As you think, those thoughts are sent out into the Universe, and they magnetically attract all like things that are on the same frequency. Everything sent out returns to the source. And that source is you.

The law of attraction doesn't care whether you perceive something to be good or bad, or whether you don't want it or whether you do want it. It's responding to your thoughts. So if you're looking at a mountain of debt, feeling terrible about it, that's the signal you're putting out into the Universe. 'I feel really bad because of all this debt I've got.' You're just affirming it to yourself. You feel it on every level of your being. That's what you're going to get more of.

The law of attraction is a law of nature. It is impersonal and it does not see good things or bad things. It is receiving your thoughts and reflecting back to you those thoughts as your life experience. The law of attraction simple gives you whatever it is you are thinking about.

The law of attraction is really obedient. When you think of the things that you want, and you focus on them with all of your intention, then the law of attraction will give you exactly what you want, every time. The law of attraction is not biased to 'want or 'don't wants'. When you focus on something, no matter what it happens to be, you really are calling that into existence. When you focus your thoughts on something you want, and you hold that focus, you are in that moment summoning what you want with the mightiest power in the Universe.

'... His whole life changed because he changed from focusing on what he did not want, what he was afraid of, what he wanted to avoid, to focusing on what he did want. His life changed because the changed his thoughts. He emitted a different frequency out into the Universe. His new thoughts became his new frequency.'

Your life is in your hands. No matter where you are now, no matter what has happened in your life, you can begin to consciously choose your thoughts, and you can change your life. There is no such thing as a hopeless situation. Every single circumstance of your life can change. You attract to you the predominant thoughts that you're holding in your awareness, whether those thoughts are conscious or unconscious.

You can see the law of attraction everywhere. You draw everything to yourself. The people, the job, the circumstances, the health, the wealth, the debt, the joy, the car that you drive, the community you're in. And you've drawn them all to you, like a magnet. What you think about, you bring about. Your whole life is a manifestation of the thoughts that go on in your head.

This is a Universe of inclusion, not exclusion. Nothing is excluded from the law of attraction. Your life is a mirror of the dominant thoughts you think. Humans have a mind that can discern. They can use their free will to choose their thoughts. They have the power to intentionally think and create their entire life with their mind.

People who have drawn wealth into their lives think thoughts of abundance and wealth, and they do not allow any contradictory thoughts to take root in their minds. Their predominant thoughts are of wealth. They only know wealth, and nothing else exists in their minds. Whether they are aware of it or not, their predominant thoughts of wealth are what brought wealth to them.

You may know of people who acquired massive wealth, lost it all, and within a short time acquired massive wealth again. What happened in these cases, whether they knew it or not, is that their dominant thoughts were on wealth; that is how they acquired it in the first instance. Then they allowed fearful thoughts of losing the wealth to enter their minds, until those fearful thoughts of loss became their dominant thoughts. They tipped the scales from thinking thoughts of wealth to thinking thoughts of loss, and so they lost it all. Once they had lost it, however, the fear of loss disappeared, and they tipped the scales back with dominant thoughts of wealth. And wealth returned.

What most people don't understand is that a thought has a frequency. We can measure a thought. So that if you're thinking that thought over and over and over again, if you're imagining in your mind having that brand new car, having the money that you need, building that company, finding your soul mate… if you're imagining what that looks like, you're emitting that frequency on a consistent basis. Thoughts are sending out that magnetic signal that is drawing the parallel back to you.

We understand that a television station's transmission tower broadcasts via a frequency, which is transformed into pictures on your television. Most of us don't really understand how it works, but we know that each channel has a frequency, and when we tune into that frequency we see the pictures on our television. We choose that frequency by selecting the channel, and we then receive the pictures broadcast on that channel. If we want to see different pictures on our television, we change the channel and tune into a new frequency.

You are a human transmission tower. You are transmitting in a frequency with your thoughts.

The pictures you receive from the transmission of your thoughts are not on a television screen in your living room, they are the pictures of your life. Your thoughts create the frequency, they attract like things on that frequency, and they are broadcast back to you as your life pictures. If you want to change anything in your life, change the channel and change the frequency by changing your thoughts.

Thoughts become things. You become, and attract, what you think.

The broken record

During the first eighteen years of our lives, we have been told 'no' about 100,000 times. How often you were told what you can do, or what you can accomplish in life?

This negative programming has come from our parents, brothers, teachers, school mates, associates, lifemates, advertising, the papers and the TV. Seventy percent of everything we think is negative, counterproductive, and works against us. Seventy-five percent of all illnesses are self-induced. We take everything to heart. Year after year, word by word, that's how our self-image was created. In time, we ourselves joined in. We began to believe that what we were being told by others – and what we were telling ourselves – was true. Repetition is a convincing argument. In time we became what we most believed about ourselves. Unless the programming we received is erased or replaced, it will stay with us and affect and direct everything we do for the rest of our lives.

By an incredibly complex physiological mechanism, a joint effort of body, brain and mind, we become the living result of our own thoughts.

How much of what you do is dependent on the conditioning, the programming you received from others and you bought and kept giving yourself? How successful you will be at anything is inexorably tied to the words and beliefs about yourself that you have stored in your subconscious mind. That was decided for us by someone else.

Think for a moment what you might do differently tomorrow if you were someone else. Or what might you do differently if you had been brought up with a completely different, more positive set of attitudes and beliefs and feelings from those which you may have now – attitudes and beliefs and feelings which in every case would assure you of having an abundance of self-belief, enthusiasm, and achievement.

You will become what you think about most

Your success or failure, large or small, will depend on what you accept from others, and what you say when you talk to yourself.

Again, what we think, is what we become.

We control with our minds most everything in our lives: our careers, health, personal relationships, our futures.

Neither luck nor desire have the slightest thing to do with it. It makes no difference whether we believe something or not. The brain simply believes what you tell it most. And what you tell it about you, it will create. It has no choice.

Self-Jive Talking

Self talking is mostly unconscious or goes unnoticed and not surprisingly, self-defeating and counter-productive.

The subconscious mind does not see the difference between the statement that we are clumsy and the statement that we are graceful, well-coordinated, and in control. It does not know the difference between being told that we are poor, and the statement that we are wealthy. It accepts our programming.

When we state, 'No matter what I do, I just can't seem to make enough money to make ends meet' our unconscious mind says, 'Okay, I'll do what you're telling me to do. I'll make sure you can't make ends meet'. It will then unleash its powerful control over our mental and physical selves to achieve the result it was told to accomplish.

Through a complex process of electrochemical physiological controls, our personal computer will affect and influence what we do, from how we get along with someone at home, to the amount of money we earn.

What we put into our brains is what we will get back out. The subconscious mind is a sponge. It will believe anything you tell it – it will even believe a lie – if you tell it often enough and strongly enough. The brain makes no moral judgments, it simply accepts what you tell it. The desktop computer doesn't care what is programmed into it. It never questions whether you are telling it the truth or not. It just accepts and acts upon whatever you program into it. The brain doesn't care! And the brain and the mind never sleep.

Most of what seems to happen to you, happen because of you – something you created, directed, influenced, or allowed to happen. Something you did (or did not do) was the cause of that success or failure.

Responsibility

Personal responsibility is at the root of everything we think, do, conceive, fail at, or achieve in our lives. It does not mean 'duty' or 'burden'. It is not the measure of our liability or our accountability: it is the basis of our individual determination to accept life and to fulfil ourselves within it.

We take our first breath by ourselves. And we take our last breath alone. How is it then that somewhere in between, in that time we call life, we expect someone to do our breathing for us?

Personal responsibility is the essence of self. By not taking responsibility for your own thoughts, we leave our minds open to the whims of others.

Through some natural law of cause and effect, when we improve ourselves, the things we would like to have in our lives follow naturally. The more successful you become inside, the more success you will automatically create on the outside.

When we want to improve ourselves in some way, we need to consider three resources: time, energy, and mind. For any self-improvement concept to be successful, it has to be simple. It has to be easy to use. And when put into practice, it has to work!

Silent self-talk is that subtle shift in your attitude from ever again looking at things in a negative way, to looking at everything in a more positive, productive way.

The limits of our income are set by our own internal beliefs. If you want to earn more, you have to start by seeing yourself as worthy, deserving, capable, and willing. Begin by giving yourself three weeks of self-talk for self-worth and financial worth – then set your goals and write your plan. Start with your programming; the rest will follow.

Setting goals and working at reaching them, is part and parcel to becoming healthy, wealthy, and wise.

Give life to your dreams, give strength to your visions, give light to your path. Grant your journey the assurance of a safe arrival. Set your goals, work at achieving them, and talk to yourself everyday along the way.

We can learn to motivate ourselves. We can learn to become self-starters, doers, and achievers. We need only to begin, and our inner selves, the part of us that wants to achieve, will soon begin to follow. There is a sleeping giant within us. It seeks and needs the motivation that comes from us. It will become a part of us which will conquer our fears, slay the dragons, and carry us on to our victories. It is a magical genie of mental powers, impatiently waiting for its release. It is the essential, self-fulfilling part of each of us. It has been waiting a long time for us to tell it what to do. Let the giant loose. Tomorrow morning, wake it up.

Mind/brain researchers have gained insight into the process of the effect of the natural chemicals our brains trigger and dump into our systems – just from a minute or two of negative emotional stress. A few minutes of anger, anxiety, negative stress, and frustration can literally toxify our physical systems for hours.

It is a self-generating cycle: thought, emotional response, physiological response, thought, emotional response, and so on, until something breaks or changes the cycle. That is why one negative incident, first thing in the morning, can cause a chain reaction which, if left unchecked, can affect everything else throughout the day. It affects our energy and our enthusiasm, our initiative and our spirit. You can successfully scuttle an entire day by allowing even a single event to create the first step in a negative cycle. This negative cycle is not caused by the problem or event – the cycle begins with how you respond to the problem.

I Got Rhythm

Take one thing at a time. Talk things out calmly and objectively. Never allow anyone or anything to push you. Get into a go-ahead, rhythmic, and unhurried pace. Keep impatience down, and consistently practise the 'easy does it' psychology. It is vital in the cure of uptightness.

Take an emergency leisurely, that is to say, let nothing make you hot and bothered. Cool it, always cool it. Think and react slowly and in leisurely fashion. Quick reaction can often lead to ill-conceived action. Leisurely procedure gives time for emotion to cool and rational insight to take over. Silence is the element in which great things fashion themselves together. Reflection upon that profound thought can lead you into the essence of creative quietness.

The ability to relax and not to be uptight and tense, the great capacity to cool it under any and all circumstances no matter how critical, depends upon long practice and determined cultivation. Proficiency may not and, indeed, does not come easily, but it comes if subjected to perseverance. Avoid the notion that you can achieve strong emotional control simply by reading a book, or by ten easy lessons. The emotions, especially if they have been treated permissively, are not easily brought under control. But the fact is that the human being can develop any desired thought pattern if he strongly wills to do so, and assiduously cultivates it.

The non-uptight person is a sound and sensible type of individual who has an objective in life, who knows what he wants to do and just goes on doing it. He lets nothing agitate or disturb him unduly. Thoroughly in control of himself mentally and emotionally, he goes along at an unhurried, orderly pace, on his way all the way.

Practise the getting of tranquility by passing peaceful words and thoughts through your mind daily and nightly. They have a strange healing quality.

Reduce as many of the noise decibels from your environment as possible. Look inside and get at the deeper cause of your nervous tension. Eradicate any unhealthy attitude pattern which is keeping you stirred up in your deep unconscious. Unhurry yourself.

Motivation that really motivates

You never know what a person has in him, until you apply dynamic and creative motivation to him. Every human being can be triggered. Indeed, every person can be opened up to more effective performance, when the combination is found that swings wide the door to let the real personality emerge.

Keep thinking, keep interested, keep praying, keep dreaming. Be mentally sensitive at all times, so that the magic word may one day speak to your deep inner self. And when it does, you want your lines of communication to be open. Imagine, pray, have faith, positive thinking, enthusiasm and inspired motivation. You can change your thinking and thereby change your life. You can do this by deliberately forcing into your subconscious vital ideas, positive images, instead of negative ones. You are constantly in a state of becoming. You become what you think. This philosophy does not mean, of course, that your life will be without problems. What it means is that you will be able to meet strength and the know-how to face it. You need only ask - and believe. Image and believe. Work and believe.

Sometimes motivation comes in the form of hard knocks, hard blows. You face roadblocks and some really tough experiences. This causes some to fold up and give up. But to others, trouble is an incentive that motivates them to harder thinking and harder working. Adversity causes some men to break; others to break records.

The most powerful motivation is spiritual motivation. Expose yourself to the spiritual. Associate with motivational people. Cultivate motivational ideas; in adversity, keep motivated, for often the best comes from difficulty. Imagine your goal. Hold that image in consciousness. Keep that image always before you, and your goal will materialise.

Anyone can handle their difficulties when they really learn to trust themselves. Have confidence. People become really quite remarkable when they start thinking that they can do things. And those who have learned to have a realistic, non-egotistical belief in themselves, who possess a deep and sound self-confidence, are assets to mankind, for they transmit their dynamic quality to those lacking it.

Creative anticipation

The trouble with some people is that subconsciously they always expect the worst to happen, so that their minds tend to image and then to create a failure situation. They must be taught confidently to image and expect the best. The practice of creative anticipation should teach them to believe in their own potential. What you deeply expect, you tend to get. Habitual expectations attract corresponding circumstances and events.

In all thinking and in all action, just as in the precise laws of mathematics and physics, all things are governed by cause and effect. Do a certain thing in a certain way and you get a certain result.

Everything in this world proceeds accordingly to law, including thought itself. We can improve ourselves by the use of applicable laws, one of which is the law of creative anticipation, or self-belief. Human beings can alter their lives by altering their attitudes of mind. The individual who mentally visualizes himself achieving rather than failing, and who is willing to pay the price of intense study and sustained effort, advances towards his goal. That mental vision is vital, for what we become is closely related to our basic self-image. What we think, what we visualize, what we image, is to a large degree what we are bound to become.

Never let a mistake cause you to stop believing in yourself, because everything passes if you let it pass, and do not hold onto it mentally.

A person learns and grows by trial and error. It just isn't possible that anybody could get by forever without making mistakes, and perhaps occasionally some costly ones. But men who really do things are those who take hold of themselves, derive some new know-how from the errors, accept the consequences, pick up the pieces, and get going. Over-zealousness to avoid mistakes can actually work against success. Some mistakes originate from an error pattern in one's thinking, while others are due to inexperience. When you repeatedly make the same mistakes, then it is a fair assumption that you may be mistake-prone. In that case a psychological study of your attitudes and reactions may be indicated. The important thing is to profit from mistakes. Just as we may learn from our success (how to do it), so also we can learn from our mistakes (how not to do it).

A person possesses within himself considerable potential. People do have within them more talent, more ability, more effective functioning than has been apparent. If we did all the things we are capable of doing we would literally astound ourselves.

No normal human being is lacking in creative potential. No matter what difficulty or crisis affect your situation, you can handle it if you think you can. Thinking positively about your ability tends to release positive mental forces that produce effective action.

Never think of yourself as failing; that is most dangerous, for the mind always tries to complete what it pictures. Instead, stamp indelibly on your mind a mental picture of yourself succeeding.

Perhaps nothing so plagues and harasses human beings as the crippling, misery-producing feeling of personal inadequacy. The cure begins when you decide that you really want to change, when you become very determined. You never really know what you can do until you try. Whenever a negative thought about yourself comes to mind, deliberately voice a positive thought to cancel it out. Do not build up obstacles in your imagination. Depreciate every so-called obstacle. Minimize them. Difficulties must be studied to be eliminated, but they should be seen realistically only for what they are. Never inflate them by fear-thoughts.

Refuse right now to believe there are things you cannot do. Some of the greatest things in this world have been accomplished by men and women who never knew what they couldn't do. Not knowing, they just went right ahead and did it.

Cut the word 'impossible' out of your mind. Eliminate it from your conversation, drop it from your thoughts, erase it from your attitudes. Get rid of it. Get through it. Stop rationalizing it. Cease excusing for it. Let that word and that concept go for good, and substitute for it that bright and shining word 'possible', which is to say - you can if you think you can. When something is considered impossible, it actually represents ignorance of the facts. It is the passing along of an error, lacking in substance.

If you are faced by a problem, and are harassed by the impossibility concept, begin a factual, objective study of the so-called impossible factors in the situation. The verdict 'impossible' is usually derived from an emotional reaction to the problem, and it can often be overcome by substituting a cool, unemotional, intellectual examination of the elements involved.

It cannot be overemphasized that myths always give way to facts. Get on with the facts. Bypass the myths. Reassert and reaffirm the fact that by the application of creative thinking you can eliminate the impossible.

Some people settle for defeat all too easily. Others do not settle easily, but trouble and failure gradually wear them down, and eventually they become tired and discouraged and give up. It's the individual who has a deep faith and gut courage who comes through life's tough battles with a victory instead of a defeat.

Courage can be many things, but the secret of courage is simply and honestly to admit your feelings of failure. And then go on and do your job in spite of them. If you wait for the perfect moment when all is safe and assured, it may never arrive. Mountains will not be climbed, races won or lasting happiness achieved.

Fear and Faith

There are many kinds of fears, from agoraphobia to claustrophobia to acrophobia. Worry affects the circulation, the heart, the glands, the whole nervous system, and profoundly affects the heart. The reason why worry kills more people than work, is that more people worry than work.

There are two massive thought forces competing for control of the mind: fear and faith, and faith is stronger – much stronger. Hold that thought of faith's greater power until you believe it, for it can be the difference not only between success and failure, but perhaps even between life and death. You do not need to be controlled by fear. The power of faith can drive off fear. When we have faith and trust, we find that this mystic and seemingly unsubstantial factor actually holds up: faith releases unsuspected powers. Learn to live with that powerful reality called faith, for faith is your friend, not your enemy.

Determine never to be pushed around by your fears. Stand up to them mentally and deny them the power to dominate you, even in the less dramatic lives most of us live.

Fear must be dealt with, so deal with it – take action. Positive, forthright action. When you are afraid of something, do not let yourself be hung up in imaginings concerning it; rather, take summary action; attack – hit it hard. The harder you strike, the more quickly and surely the fear will subside.

It is a fact that much fear currently manifesting itself may be traced to one's childhood experience. To deal with it effectively, professional and expert counselling may in some cases be indicated.

Chronic anxiety often stems from fears contracted in childhood through the power of suggestibility. Another big cause is a sense of guilt that develops. Counselling can bring the sufferer to see the connection between his fears and his guilt - and thereby motivate him to a moral housecleaning. Self-knowledge is the beginning of wisdom. Often it is also the beginning of a cure. Old fears must be replaced with something positive – a strong faith – else they recur or new fears take their place. We pick up fear from those around us who would not for all the world do anything to harm us. But unconsciously fears are projected upon children, who thereafter must suffer and struggle with this strange malady unless, by right thinking, by professional assistance, and by acquiring a healthy-minded faith, they find deliverance and relief.

In overcoming fear it is important to be free of all mental conflict so that you are able to approach situations with normal naturalness. Take every proper precaution. Have faith in god, in yourself, and in people. Then just go about your job normally and without fear.

Make miracles happen

When anyone starts expecting a miracle, he presently becomes so conditioned in mind, that he begins actually making miracles happen. He gets on the 'miracle wavelength'. His native abilities become focused positively rather than negatively. Creative forces are released in his mind. The flow-away of values is checked and reversed. Life now flows not away from him, but towards him. The negative expectations which drove away the good are replaced by positive expectations which attract the good.

Demosthenes said that small opportunities are often the beginning of great enterprises. Walt Disney was rejected a lot of times in his youth. Back in those days when he scarcely had two coins to rub together, and everyone was giving him the brush-off, Disney could have become soured on the 'establishment', growling that the country was for the rich only, and the system had to be destroyed. But this man didn't go emotional and become a bitter militant. He just kept on believing in himself, and working and dreaming and making miracles happen, and becoming world's master of childhood fantasy.

Law of Successful Achievement

The first law is to have a goal; not a vague, fuzzy goal, but a sharply focused objective. You must know what you want to do and where you want to go, what you want to be. And have no doubt about it. The next step, and it's a real practical one, is to pray about this goal to be sure it is a right objective; because if it isn't right, it's wrong, and nothing wrong ever turned out right.

Then hold the goal tenaciously in the conscious mind until, by a process of intellectual osmosis, it sinks into the subconscious, and when it becomes firmly fixed in the subconscious, you have it, because it has you, all of you - your hopes, your thoughts, your efforts. Then put positive thoughts behind your goal. The negative thinker lets loose destructive forces that can destroy him. In sending out negative thoughts, he activates the world around him negatively. Following the law of attraction, the negative thinker tends to draw back to himself negative results: he attracts them. Change negative to positive thoughts every time they appear.

Motivated goals and miracles can come true. Miracles are of all sizes: big ones, medium-sized ones, and small ones. If you start believing in little miracles, you can work up to the bigger ones. Think and believe and work and treat people right, and give it all you've got, and you will find yourself doing the most amazingly constructive things in this life.

But the self-minimiser will never do wonders or work miracles. Since he is appraising himself and his opportunities on a low-level basis, it is to such a basis, pathetically, that he is condemning himself. Since thoughts tend to reproduce themselves in kinds, the dismal thinker is likely to come up with dismal results, whereas the person who thinks hopefully can be expected to attract constructive results.

Miracles are not altogether made out of dreams. Often they are put together out of plain, everyday, nonglamorous facts. Just wanting to do something with life and with yourself goes a long way towards getting a miracle going. That urge to be something and do something, to move ahead, to climb up, to get more meaning into life, is the stuff out of which miracles are made.

Thousands of individuals have discovered or rediscovered, vast store-houses of imaginative power within themselves by deliberating putting down ideas in a piece of paper. The powerful principle is think first, judge later. Put down each and every idea or notion that occurs to you. As you jot down your ideas, an idea will trigger others. Your associative processes, which are the heart of your creative power, will function more rationally, if given free rein.

The way to have a good idea is to have a lot of ideas. Significantly more good ideas can be produced by applying the deferred judgement principle.

From the comment of a successful miracle maker to a beginner: 'You are an intelligent and educated person, and I just won't believe that you are totally devoid of skills. There is an idea lurking in your mind, which we are going to find, one which will open up a terrifically exciting life for you. So let's put down every idea we can think of in a brain-storming session and see what we come up with.' Keep probing for the tremendous quality built into you which has not yet emerged.

Always be on the lookout for the big idea that can change your life. Know that you are yourself a miracle. Believe you can make miracles happen - by thinking, praying, believing, working, and by helping people.

Boredom

There is no need to be bored or frustrated or fed up. Life can be exciting. Day after day, all the way, your life can be packed full of meaning. The ecstasy and the happiness are experienced by getting on top of your problems, by recovering from your failures, by putting meaning into the routine. People who are really organised, who think straight, who are in control of their attitudes and have exciting motivations, are never bored.

The seemingly increase in boredom can be directly traced to our easy way of living. We don't get enough out-and-out tough physical exercise the way our forefathers did. We've become spectator sportsmen. Monotony may surround us all, but the problem is within the individual. Life is a single case of being scared much of the time – or being bored. Furthermore, if life is too easy, it's no fun. We've made it too easy for our kids as well.

The bored, the frustrated, those who have had it and are fed up, would do well to get away from cities which are increasingly dirty and frightful with noise, and get reacquainted with the great natural world. It is mental exhilaration that knocks out boredom, eliminates frustration, and kicks the fed-up feeling for good. The more you are into things, the greater the zest. The more active the mind is, the better it will perform, and the longer it will keep on performing. To slow down can result in boredom, but not if one continues to exercise the mind by reading, thinking, and by participating in contemporary affairs. You can avoid boredom all your life, if you keep alive mentally all your life. Keep thinking, keep moving, keep participating.

A clean mind always delivers power. If power is not being delivered, it might be that someone does not a have a clean mental engine. May be it would be as well to use some intellectual detergent to flush out of the mind those old, tired, listless, debilitating thoughts of inferiority, resentment, and negativism. This process might get the mental engine clean, so that it could produce maximum power.

One quality which often impedes the exercise of judgment and may actually set it aside, is an uncontrolled emotional reaction to people and situation.

Mental control is the secret of mature and creative judgement. Your mind is an instrument designed to serve you, not to destroy you. When uncontrolled, your mind can be very damaging to you, but when controlled it can develop unlimited power.

Discover the basic principles of successful achievement; mentally turn away from your failures. Know yourself. Control your mind. Think. Make right decisions. Never accept defeat. Believe in yourself. Mentally accept your great future. Never think of failing. Believe that you can if you think you can.

'I am not interested in the past. I am interested only in the future, for that is where I expect to spend the rest of my life.'

Concentrate on the fact that your future is not determined by circumstances over which you have no control, but by proper mental outlook over which you do have control. You truly can shape your own future. How do you get that right mental outlook? Start developing rightness in thinking. Start siphoning off the error in your mind. For error results in wrong thinking, which in turn results in wrong action, which produces wrong outcomes. The only remedy for error is rightness. This requires a quality of study and thought, that will in time develop keener insight and perceptiveness. The better outlook will create the conditions of a better future.

Since the mind is a vast reservoir of needed resources, it follows that any kind of foreign matter that may block off the orderly flow of those resources, will need to be eliminated. No doubt the explanation of much frustration and failure may be attributed to those blocks to the free passage of creative thought, which have been permitted to lodge in the mind. The tremendous resources needed to accomplish the job well, or even to live well, are dammed up and cannot get through.

If only

The trouble with 'if only' if that it doesn't change anything. It keeps the person facing the wrong way – backwards instead of forwards. It wastes time. If you let it become a habit, it can become a real roadblock, an excuse for not trying any more. Shift focus. Change 'if only' with 'next time'. The 'if only' attitude leads to a dull and uninspired reaction to things. But 'next time' signifies a positive and courageous attack on problems. Live a day at a time and do a job at a time. Then go on to the next time. Unhappily, lots of people live in the past, present and future all at the same time. What an error to waste mental energy brooding over past events, or worrying about problems that might develop at some future time, and then again might not. The successful person learns to live in the present only, but always headed towards next time.

Never get hung-up on 'if only'. Forget it, and get ready for the next time. If you carry around in your mind from one day to the next a load of dejection, because things haven't gone as well as you had hoped, you will run completely out of energy. Finish every day, and be done with it. You have done what you could. Some blunders and absurdities no doubt crept in; forget them as soon as you can. Tomorrow is a new day; begin it well and serenely and with too high a spirit to be cumbered with our old nonsense. This day is all that is good and fair. It is too dear, with its hopes and invitations, to waste a moment on yesterdays.

What a person can be and what he can do is largely determined by the degree of self-limitation which he mentally imposes on himself. If he images himself on a restrictive level, the flow of resources from the mind will be reduced and maintained at a trickle of the full potential. A certain degree of boldness if required of the individual who wishes to make more of himself. Boldness is an activator of power from the mind. Go at it boldly, and you'll find unexpected forces closing around you and coming to you and the mind, ever the willing servant, will respond to boldness, for boldness is a command to deliver mental resources. Boldly expect, and the power will come through. The tests of life are to make, not break, us.

Believe that you have inherent in your mind all the resources you will ever need. Build up your resources inventory by faith and know-how.

Remember that spiritual power activates your forces of mind and spirit.

Never minimize your ability to think your way through any situation. If power isn't coming through, find the block and remove it.

Keep alert for those flashes of insight which come when you're really thinking.

Skip 'if only'; concentrate on 'next time'.

Be bold, and mighty powers will come to your aid.

Changing a thought pattern is no easy process. Sick thoughts, negative thoughts, thoughts of resentment, of hate, inferiority, wear a 'groove' into the consciousness that isn't quickly overcome. One might wish for some magic pill to heal these maladies, but perhaps that would not be best even if it were possible. It could be that health of personality is better served by struggle and discipline and the curative practice of thought reversal.

Emotional tensions, emotional stress and strains, may produce chronic depression and fatigue with the lowering of bodily resistance to infection and disease. Prolonged anxiety and worry, uncontrolled passion and temper, the high pressure and tempo of present-day life, will bring on degenerative changes in the heart, kidneys, liver and other vital organs, together with hypertension and arteriosclerosis. Hate and fear can poison the body as much as any toxic chemicals.

Healthy thinking can be a vitality-producing process. Such thoughts help to keep the body in balance and functioning in a normal manner. Think defeat and you will tend to create the circumstances that lead to defeat. Think inadequacy and you may ultimately fail to perform in an adequate manner. But if you think victory and success – really think it, really believe it – then you will tend to perform in a manner that leads to such an outcome. Similarly, in the matter of well-being, positive results come from visualizing yourself as a whole. See your mind and body as strong and vital and they will tend to become as you imagine them.

Healthy thinking is increasingly recognized as an important factor in well-being. Years ago a doctor might depend upon medicine only. But because man is a unity – body, mind and spirit, and psyche and the soma are closely related, scientific thought treatment is generally considered entirely relevant to the healing process.

One Day in Your Life

Thousands of people are making themselves ill and encouraging other maladies and diseases by unhealthy thinking. The solution is to affirm the life force; drop uptightness; cast out all hate; emphasize love. The most curative thought in the world is the thought of love. Go around loving people; thinking good thoughts about everyone. Cast out all negative thoughts and fill the mind with positive thoughts. Healthy-mindedness makes people healthy, vital and alive. Try living one day without any unhealthy thoughts. Help the doctor by thinking healthy thoughts. Think health, practice health, pray health. See yourself as a whole person. Practice easing your way along. Do your best; take it as it comes. You can handle anything if you think you can. Just keep cool, and keep your sense of humour going. Practice 'self-possession': to possess yourself, never let your controlled self get out of control. Practice serenity and urbanity. Keep your emotions in balance, keep them level; keep your sense of humour above those who think all civilization began this morning, and that everything has to be settled right away, now, before tonight.

The wisdom of equanimity is based on a sense-of-humour reaction about all human activity. The person who masters this quality is bound to enjoy life far better than the excitable and super-concerned, eager-beaver type. Equanimity conjures the picture of a person who, no matter what, remains poised, in perfect balance, inwardly controlled, indeed one who is able to ease up and maintain a sense of humour. This philosophy may be stated as: 'So what?' Even this will pass away. Don't take any event, any turmoil, or even yourself, too seriously. Employ your sense of humour, take it easy, and wait it out, for nothing lasts forever. The past is a great invention; it mercifully swallows up all those tensed-up, so-called 'immediate' matters.

Many people fail to do creative jobs in the world, not because they are not capable enough, but because they push it too hard; they overpress. The secret of efficiency is to think and plan and give the project all that one has of constructive effort, and then rest it; don't overpress it; relax; ease up.

Do not take yourself too seriously, but believe in yourself completely. Work diligently. Think creatively. Do all possible to insure a successful outcome. Apply intelligent thought in depth. Do your homework. Never overpress. Ease up. You have done all that you can. Let it work out. It will, and much better than if you keep fussing with it.

Imperturbable, serene, urbane, never letting anything rile you, letting nothing disturb you, taking things as they come, with equanimity, is vital to successful living. Only the person who performs in this manner is able to achieve the philosophical cast of mind that can surmount current tension and stress. Then, no matter how much may be thrown at him, his inner quality of equanimity and imperturbability can ride it out.

Persevere and hope. It is better to hope than despair. To keep hope going, it is important to get on top of things mentally; to know that you can if you think you can, in whatever situation that confronts you. If you get on top of your problems, so that you are less looking down rather than up at them, you have a tactical advantage over difficulty. To keep hope going is important also because it stimulates comeback power, and we must all have comeback power to live in this world. When you become mentally convinced that you can make a comeback from any adversity, then all of your creative forces will come to your aid. Never think that you've had it, or that you are through. 'The tide always comes back'. No matter the failures or defeats. They can be reversed. The attitude of expecting the return of good days after a difficult experience serves to motivate comeback.

The Miracle of Change

A miracle is a phenomenon not presently explainable by scientific formula, but which is validated by the spiritual formula of positive faith.

When the rock is hard, we get harder than the rock. When the job is tough, we get tougher than the job.

The 'if' thinker broods over a difficulty or a setback, saying to himself, 'If I had done this or that…', 'If the circumstances had been different…', 'If others had not treated me so unfairly…' So it goes from one weak explanation or rationalization to another, round and round, getting nowhere.

The 'how' thinker wastes no energy on post-mortems when trouble or even disaster hits him. He immediately looks for the best solution, for he knows there is always a solution. He asks himself, 'How can I use this setback creatively? How can I work something good out of this? How can I stage a comeback?' Not 'if', but 'how'.

One of the first secrets of change is to recognize and trust our ability to make a change and to sustain it. If we do not believe, then we cannot even attempt to change, and will not discover our new abilities to create miracles. On this basis of belief, by understanding how miracles occur, we can immediately begin to use our inner potential and create the changes we seek.

Procrastination ranks highest on the list of blocks that hold people back. All life is dynamic and requires change, and life today is much faster than ever before. By applying a few new principles for making a change, life can genuinely be easier. Suddenly, instead of struggling and suffering, we find ourselves effortlessly flowing through life, making the necessary adjustments not just to cope, but to make our dreams come true.

Miracles occur all the time, but we normally just call it luck. Attributing our success to luck, implies that we have no control over the good fortune we experience. The truth is, there are reasons why good things happen. Choices are made, and the results come. When good results come and we don't know how we did it, then we call it luck. We call it luck only because we don't clearly understand how our beliefs, feelings, thoughts, attitudes, choices, and actions determine all the results we get in life.

Through learning the way people think, feel, and so on, prior to a miracle or 'lucky event', we can learn how to start creating practical miracles in our own lives.

Rather than wonder, 'Does miraculous healing really occur?' we would do better to ask, 'How and why does faith heal, and why is it sometimes temporary?' Then we can ask, 'What can be done so that illness or problems don't return?'

The temporary nature of miracle healing, transformations, or changes is the placebo effect. Often patients will get better simply because they believe they will. The sheer belief that they are being treated for their problem or condition creates temporary healing.

The placebo effect appears in other situations as well. People will listen to a motivational speaker or preacher, and suddenly be inspired to make positive changes to increase success or love more fully. It is not unusual for people who order exercise equipment to rarely use their products after a few weeks. Many never open the box. What equipment do you have around the house that you are not using?

For most of us, enthusiasm fades fast. While some people continue ordering the next quick fix, others are quick to mistrust or dismiss miraculous claims. As with any other placebo, if we believe, the miracle will begin… but belief is not enough to sustain it.

Many people experience the placebo effect in matters of love. When they first meet someone, they are overcome with emotion. We are certain we have found the person of our dreams and we fall in love. Ironically, when we fall in love it is often with someone we don't even know, or with whom we have had very little interaction. Abruptly all our loneliness and pain disappears, at least for a while, this is why falling in love can be such a relief. It also explains why falling out of love can be such a letdown. When we stop believing our partner is the one, all our past unresolved pain that was relieved by falling in love suddenly returns.

The problem with believing and being repeatedly disappointed, is that we stop believing we can get what we need, and that we can make our dreams come true.

When we stop believing in the possibility of positive change, then we have no power to change. Optimism is the basis of lasting inspiration. Without hope, we have no motivation. We resign ourselves to the limited belief that this is as good as it gets. While there is a certain comfort in this acceptance, there is no passion, and there are no miracles.

Developing the power to create practical miracles doesn't mean that you can do anything, or cause anything to happen. Just because more is possible, it doesn't mean that anything is possible, and this is the point: More is possible.

Even with miraculous power, you cannot make all relationships work. You cannot please everyone, or be pleased by everyone. You could be in the right relationship and still struggle, because you are not using your miraculous potential to create lasting love. You could be in the right career, and still fail to succeed, only because you are not using your miraculous power to increase success. You could be eating healthy foods and doing exercise and cultivating your spirit, but if you are not using your miraculous power to create vibrant health, you may still get sick.

Everything we observe is miraculous. When your finger is cut and the body begins healing itself, it is a miracle. Yet, as soon as these miracles become common to our experience, we stop seeing them as miracles.

All addictions ultimately come from being overly dependent on someone or something outside of yourself to be happy. If you are dependent on your partner to feel good, then when you give, some part of you needs and hopes to get something in return. Couples who primarily come together to fill up, and not to give, are always disappointed. The act of giving is eventually not as fulfilling, because they are still dependent on receiving before they can feel good. We naively expect perfection, which does not exist. Ultimately, instead of feeling energized by giving, we become tired, empty, and exhausted. Whenever you feel resentment, it is a sign that you were giving to get something in return, rather than giving from a sense of fullness without expectations or demands.

Rather than depending on your partner to feel good, view him or her as a good dessert. You – not your partner – are responsible for supplying the important nutrients in your life. By loving yourself and having a fulfilling life first, the extra love your partner provides is an added bonus that you are not dependent on.

Out and About Love

Women often think that they are giving without expecting something in return, but after a few years of feeling neglected in a relationship, they will complain, 'I have given so much and have gotten nothing in return.' The mistake is not in giving to her partner, but rather in not taking the time to give to herself, so that she is free to give to her partner without demanding more in return. It is amazing how much more willing men are to give, when they are asked for more in a nondemanding or nonresentful manner. The secret to enjoying more of what our partner has to offer, is first to give to ourselves whatever we need, so that we are not dependent or demanding change from our partner.

Healing Strategy

Sometimes before a physical sickness clears up, an emotional issue must be healed. At other times, a person can make a life change or change of habit first, and then the emotional issues begin to surface in order to be healed (like resistance). Or, it may be that first the emotional issue becomes healed and released, and then the necessary life change becomes clear, and we are naturally motivated to make the change.

If every day we go to work because we need the money, and not because it makes us feel good, then we are disconnecting from our inner power. By not following our heart and freely choosing our work, we create our own misery and sickness. When we are free to work, not primarily for the money but because it makes us feel good, then our greatest power to change our circumstances comes forward.

This explains why some wealthy people just get richer. They work not because they need the money, but to serve others in a way that makes them feel good. When wealthy people get sick or lose their wealth, it is often because they stop working. Since they don't have to work, they lose their motivation to work. They become soft, lazy, unproductive, unhappy, sick, or experience substance abuse.

The secret of creating miracles is first to change your attitude without depending on outer circumstances to change. When you work as if money doesn't matter as much, your decisions come from your own set of values, and not from those of others. You are free to be yourself and do what your conscience and sense of duty dictates. We still need money from our work to pay our bills, but the primary reason we work is to express ourselves in service to the world in some meaningful way.

When we relax as if everything will be okay, we ground in our true selves, we are able to relax in our lives even in the midst of turmoil, helplessness, and uncertainty as if we know with certainty that everything will turn out okay. Yes, we experience loss, yes, we make mistakes, but by healing our wounds and facing our challenges with an open heart, we discover that every experience offers a growth opportunity to us. When we approach crises with inner calm, we are much more effective at finding solutions than we would be if we were experiencing anxiety and fear. Our capacity to create miracles does not change us in any way. Yet, once we are given the opportunity to identify this capacity and use it, it can be felt and increased.

Those of us who started using personal computers twenty years ago have had to suffer with slow processing speeds and limited storage space. To secure even the smallest advancement, we always had to pay dearly. Today, we buy computers at a fraction of the cost we used to pay, and these machines are not only smaller, lighter, easier to use, and light-years faster, but they are also capable of storing all the data we could ever imagine. You may have wasted your life squandering your potential, repeatedly making the same mistakes, and overlooking your inner gifts, but it is never too late to benefit from this new universal blessing. No one is denied entrance and there is no price to pay. This new inner technology is already yours.

Even spending years on a technique of inner development to access this new power doesn't give you an extra advantage. Unless you have been making lots of changes and innovations in your practice, it is probably now time to upgrade. We don't have to scrap our past; we just need to update and upgrade to access the new potential.

Religious traditions have so much to offer if we can simply reinterpret some of their restrictive and limiting aspects, and forgive their abuses and corruption. Rejecting religion is like rejecting Beethoven, just because we like pop or because Beethoven didn't play an electric guitar. Why not respect and enjoy it all?

Two thousand years ago, Jesus shocked the establishment when he said the law of God is already written in your heart. When we learn to use our potential and open our hearts, we are then not dependent on anyone but ourselves to reveal to us what is true.

Without direct experience, you certainly can have an opinion, but you cannot know. You can really never know what is right for another. As you find the truth within, you will understand the underlying message in all religions is the same, and that some messages are no longer appropriate.

By their thirties, many people have given up thinking they can change. They no longer make resolutions, because they have failed to follow through so many times before. Rather than suffer the humiliation of repeated failure, we lose our innocent exuberance to be better and happier.

In a like manner, when other people have let us down, we give up believing that change is possible. We give up trying to get the support we need. This commonly happens more clearly in intimate relationships. First we feel disappointed, then we lose hope for change. As a result, men often stop caring, while women stop trusting.

If we are not dependent on our partners for our happiness, then when they frustrate or disappoint us in some way, it is like a ripple of upset on an ocean of love, respect, appreciation, understanding, acceptance, caring, and trust. To heal overdependence, besides looking inside ourselves for fulfilment, we must also occasionally look outside the relationship for fun and friendship. It is not healthy when your mate is your only best friend, or when you always do everything together. It is important to sustain a separate life as well. When we are not so dependent on our partner for everything, we become forgiving of our partner's mistakes, and more accepting of his or her limitations and differences.

Instant Karma

The principle of instant karma is that if you are feeling really good inside, then 'instantly' the people you interact with tend to make you feel really good. If you are anxious and in a hurry, then the grocery line you pick is always the slowest line and you feel even more in a hurry. If you are angry, then people do things to make you angrier. If you feel like a victim, then people do things that make you feel more like a victim. If you begin to let go of your anger, people begin to let go of theirs.

Instant karma means that what you put out is what you get back – instantly. It implies that the whole process is speeded up. The world mirrors you right now. In the old model, if you were bad in a past life, you didn't get the right to plant corn in the next life. You had to be punished until you were worthy of getting another chance.

Karma and punishment

Every action has a consequence, but at the same time, no one ever deserves punishment. One of the practical implications of forgiveness is the letting go of our need to punish. Forgiveness of others frees us from holding on to the pain that another has caused us. When an unsafe driver's license is taken away, this is not punishment but a protection of others, until they learn to drive. Giving up punishment frees us and society to rehabilitate the offender, rather than make the problem worse. When we respond to the mistakes and the bad actions of others with the intent to punish, deprive, get even, or make someone feel guilty, it not only hurts them, but it locks us into the past as well. It serves no healthy purpose. Our justification of punishment could sound like this: 'They deserve terrible punishment because their actions will keep me from ever being happy. They must pay the price and compensate me for my pain. They have no right to be happy when I am in such pain because of what they did to me'. We are affirming our powerlessness to create a better life.

To forgive is to release the offender from any debt to us. When we forgive them, they win and we win. By letting it go, we are then free to be in the moment and start again to make the best of what happened and to move on. Focusing on what was lost or the pain that was caused, we are forced to live once again in the past.

If we believe others deserve punishment, then we believe we deserve punishment, and as a result, we will continue to punish ourselves consciously or subconsciously for the mistakes we have made. Many people are too afraid to take risks. They are so afraid to make mistakes and stain their purity, or look inadequate in some way. Most people are afraid that if they make mistakes, they will lose either love or success forever.

The truth is they may incur a loss, but it will not be forever. When you give yourself permission to experiment more and make some mistakes, you open the door for miraculous and accelerated change.

By learning to use your inner creative power, you can live in the moment and begin consciously creating the future you want. Forgiveness releases you from the influence of the past and frees you to be in the present to create something new. If someone stole your money, by forgiving him or her you are free to create even more money from the present time. If, on the other hand, you hold on to your hurt and close your heart, then you perpetuate the loss. Feeling like a victim, you continue to attract or be attracted to situations that make you feel like a victim.

The old concept of karma means your future is determined by what you have done or not done, thought or not thought, believed or not believed, felt or not felt, said or not said, promised or not promised, needed or not needed, etc. The new concept of instant karma is that your future is determined by what you do, think, and feel today, and those are now your choice.

Two thousand years ago, the grace or freedom from past karma that comes with forgiveness was incomprehensible. Although Jesus and other great teachers taught this message to the masses, most people could not understand it. This was really a new idea. Modern teachers deliver this same message of forgiveness, and finally people are getting it. We are now ready to open our hearts and experience the grace that comes when we can love again and again as if for the first time.

In the past, people were closed to their true selves and unaware of authentic feelings. They were not conscious of their inner motives, beliefs, and feelings that eventually would determine their words, actions, and results.

The magic of miracles is simply to remove the blocks that prevent us from distilling the best each situation has to offer and then move forward. Some people struggle to have a positive mood, but then wonder why people are so nasty to them. If could be people are mean to you because you are not following your soul desire, and the world is resisting you. Simply, you are swimming upstream, so naturally life is more difficult. It could also be that you are drawn to mean people in your life, to teach you understanding and tolerance. Often, when our souls want to grow, we are attracted to situations that will challenge us and make us stronger.

At each stage of life, about every seven years, a significant change occurs and a new need emerges. Without the appropriate support we require at each stage, we are unable to realize our full potential. This limitation can be overcome. As adults becoming aware of what we haven't gotten, we can take responsibility for filling the void and giving to ourselves what we didn't get before. For example, if a child doesn't get enough sleep or food, his body will not develop; not getting enough love and support to feel good about ourselves will affect and limit all later stages of development. We now have the power to give ourselves the love and support we missed, and overcome the limitations of our past. By recognising what you missed, you can awaken the suppressed or denied parts of your true self, and experience the power of creating practical miracles.

The Need for Healing

It is customary to go through a healing crisis at the beginning of each of the life stages. To the degree that people ignore their needs for healing at these junction points, they are somewhat held back from being fully successful in the next stage. Then, in the next stage their bodies may begin to get sick, their relationships may become disappointing, or their business may go downhill. In order for us to heal, we can awaken our body's healing potential by getting the support we couldn't or didn't receive when we were younger.

When inspired, happy, or energized, you are feeling the benefits of the free flow of natural energy. When stressed, pressured, anxious, or distressed, you are experiencing the symptoms of blocked natural energy. Natural energy brings greater peace, joy, confidence, love, patience, optimism, strength, humility, fulfilment, inspiration, courage, and innocence. With this kind of support, we can better focus our minds and be more creative and successful. A request for natural energy needs to be sincere and heartfelt, not to convince the energy to respond, but to make us more receptive. A vulnerable, humble, and appreciative attitude makes you more receptive to receiving this miraculous power. This energy is intelligent, it creates our bodies, digests our foods, regulates body temperature, maintains balance and equilibrium, distributes nutrients to the billions of cells in the body, regulates breathing, keeps the heart pumping twenty-four hours a day, and contracts and relaxes muscles. All we really need to do is draw it in and then direct it with our will or attention.

Modulate your Frequency

All energy travels in waves or frequencies, and each element has its own frequency band. When an element is rich and vibrant in pure natural energy, then that particular frequency is awakened in you and you can begin to access its energy. A fresh rose is one of the most healing frequencies in nature. To find comfort, some people love to sit in the sun, while others enjoy long showers. This often is because one soul needs more fire energy, while another requires more water energy.

When our hearts are open we are attracted to what we need, but when our hearts are closed, we are repelled by the elements we need most. When you are depressed you may dread going for a walk in nature, when that is just the thing you need to do. If you are really stressed, then the thought of recharging is also repelling.

Most people are unaware that, in addition to absorbing positive energy from others, we can absorb stress and distress. Children absorb a lot of their parent's stress, distress, even their pain. Quite often, one of the major causes of cancer and other life-threatening diseases is the absorption of stress. When medicine cannot help a situation, it is usually because the person's own healing power is blocked by accumulating too much stress and distress over the years. By learning to decharge, people are more effectively able to heal themselves.

Being a loving and giving person not only feels good but gives us energy. At the same time, it makes us vulnerable to picking up more stress and distress. This is not a problem, if we continue to fill up with positive energy, and are able to send back into nature any excess energy.

When we help others who are stressed or distressed, we may also receive some of their stress and distress. Any time you help someone, there is always an exchange of energy. If you happen to have less stress than another does, you will absorb part of their stress and distress as well. As they feel better from interacting with you, their stress lifts out of them and part of it travels to you. A warm room gets cooler and a cool room gets warmer when the door between them is opened.

When a singer like Barbra Streisand enchants her audience, her fans' hearts begin to open and their stress is released. A part of this stress goes to Barbra.

Unless she is prepared for this, by having support in her life to release this added stress, she will begin to suffer problems. Her normal little problems or stresses in life will suddenly seem bigger and more gripping. This simple insight explains why fame is like putting a huge magnifying glass up to our every shortcoming and limitation. At work, unless we are regularly able to release the stress we accumulate, we will eventually get sick or burn out.

When you are upset, stressed, or distressed, you are generally just overcharged with energy. The process of decharging sends out excess energy, so that your upset becomes more manageable. Things become easier if we send out excess energy. Don't feel concerned that you will lose energy. You are only sending out excess energy.

Have you ever noticed that at special occasions, when there is always a lot of energy and love, you may easily become upset or overwhelmed? This means that you need to decharge. Let Mother Nature help you out by taking a little of that energy that is overwhelming and upsetting you.

A paradoxical truth

You can never recharge too much. Recharge does not produce excess energy. When you are full, it just stops working until you use up some of that energy. We get excess energy through sharing our energy and then having more come back to us. In a very real sense, when you give your love and support to others, more energy comes back to you. When you give a lot, you will end up with excess energy. At this point you need to decharge.

Many very sick people tend to be loving people who give a lot and absorb a lot of stress and distress from others. Excess energy is clearly a major contributing factor to chronic pain and sickness. Even chronic fatigue is the result of excess energy. We feel energized when our energy is flowing. Fatigue comes from blocked energy. Besides causing stress, distress, fatigue, and pain, with excess energy the body loses its ability to heal itself, it gets weaker and weaker until it develops a life-threatening sickness.

Imagine energy could be explained in terms of watts like different sizes of light bulbs. If you have one hundred watts of peaceful energy and you absorb from the outer world two hundred watts of stressful energy, then clearly you will begin to resonate with the stressful energy, and feel stressed.

But if you had two hundred watts of peaceful energy and absorbed one hundred watts of stressful energy, then it would not affect you much. Still, having that excess energy would make you feel some increased stress.

If you had two hundred watts of peaceful energy and absorbed two hundred watts of peaceful energy, but you could only handle two hundred watts, then you would begin to feel really stressed. Little things that would not normally bother you would suddenly become big issues. Excess energy is the number one reason to overreact to situations. Decharging is the ultimate stress-management technique.

Never use this information to be afraid of stress or other people's stress levels. Just as you can absorb stress in a few minutes, you can also release it in a few minutes. The more sensitive you are, the more you will tend to gather stress. This is not a problem because if you can absorb it easily, then you can also decharge more easily. Accumulating stress only becomes a problem when you don't take time to decharge.

To increase your ability to decharge using air, do it while going on a walk or while exercising. Stagnant air can only absorb so much excess energy and that is why fresh air is recommended. It is good to open the windows for five to ten minutes to refreshen the room. You can decharge into a glass of water and then drink it. It will continue to decharge you as it moves through your body. All things that are healing, inspiring, nurturing, or relaxing can be used to decharge.

Later, add a simple phrase to very briefly put in words what you want to decharge. "Decharge my disappointment" "Decharge my anger". Be precise but keep it simple.

An old-fashioned way to deal with anger, was to go start a war or get in a fight. By expressing the excess energy that fuels the anger, it goes away, and then people make up. War, fighting, and yelling is really just an out-of-date way of decharging. This explains why male teenagers after getting in fights would then become close friends. Couples often make up after a yelling fight not because they have really resolved anything, but they have just used up their excess energy and then forget what they were fighting about.

The twelve most potent healing emotions for decharging are anger, sadness, fear, sorrow, frustration, disappointment, worry, embarrassment, rage, hurt, panic, and shame.

To benefit from the healing that occurs from recharging and decharging, it is essential that we drink lots of water. Whenever any purification occurs on the soul, mental, and emotional levels, toxins automatically are released into the body and must be eliminated. We need to drink water to wash away toxins. Also increase natural foods and remove refined and processed foods from the diet. Natural food is food that hasn't been processed to increase its shelf life in the store. Foods that will spoil right away are always the easiest for your body to digest and assimilate nutrition from.

The most important food to replace is refined sugar. The idea is first to give up your sugar addiction so that you can feel your natural hunger once again. Drinking 4 litres of water a day, along with decharging, makes it easy to give up refined sugar. When you experience increased stress or distress in your life, then automatically you will thirst for more than two litres a day. When you stop eating refined sugars, immediately your body rejoices and begins to heal itself by releasing old toxins. If you don't supply enough water for your body to wash away these toxins, you're your body becomes blocked and murky with toxins. This lowers your energy, and suddenly you feel a craving for the quick energy you get from refined sugars. By drinking four litres of water a day, your sugar cravings are easily replaced by healthy desires for natural fruit or honey. Artificial sweeteners are unhealthy, and should be avoided like rat poison. When you start craving sugar or unhealthy foods, simply drink a glass of water, practice decharging. Breathing exercises or vigorous walking can be very helpful to burn off the stress and distress being released. When you crave refined sugar, avoid fruit juices, but eat lots of whole fruit, nuts, and dates. They are great replacements for candy bar addicts. Some people have never experienced natural thirst in their lives. From the moment in infancy when they were first given bottled milk with sugar, they became addicted. If you feel your natural thirst and hunger, suddenly natural and healthy foods become incredibly delicious. Everything you eat will begin tasting better.

When we work primarily for the money, it is more difficult to feel our true needs or appreciate what we have now. When we are already happy, we don't feel an urgent need for money to make us happier. The real truth is that we always have exactly what we need to take our next step in our life's journey.

With a clearer awareness of what we really need, we more easily can stay balanced and not be swayed by the temptations of greater success. We learn that by prioritizing what is really important, we can have plenty of money and also be happy, healthy, and in love. When we suffer or feel stressed, it is because we are not recognizing that in this moment we always have everything we need to be happy. When you are not so dependent on money to make you happy, you are free to create whatever you want, including more money.

Although you cannot always control events, you can control your attitude and feelings about them. By learning to generate a positive attitude during the day, you will become a magnet attracting the success you have planned.

After spending a few minutes recharging or decharging, take a few minutes to organize your day. Think about the things you expect to happen. Next, imagine things happening a little bit better. Now you are imagining a good or better day. Next, take a leap, and imagine the best happening. As you imagine the best happening, then imagine how that would make you feel.

To get what you want, first appreciate what you have. It is only when we are relaxed and open that we can begin to recognize the endless possibilities that always exist to create positive and meaningful change.

Many people complain that they didn't get the support they needed in childhood. Rather than remain victims of our past, we can change the influence of our personal history to support us rather than hold us back. To be free of the limiting aspects of the past, we must first understand how our past can support us. A negative experience cannot be removed directly, but it can be replaced with a positive one.

When we were children, if we were loved, we developed the knowledge that we are lovable. This provides the basis for increased confidence and self-forgiveness. This ability to love ourselves is already within ourselves, but it is triggered by our parents' nurturing support. Later in life, by exploring 'What if we did get the support we missed', we are, actually, undoing the effects of the past. By exploring 'What if', we give ourselves the option to trigger and awaken our feelings of self-love.

Let's say that you have difficulty forgiving others. By going back and remembering mistakes your parents made and ask yourself, 'What if they apologized and corrected their behaviour?' you will begin to feel increasing forgiveness for them. With this ability to forgive them, you will find it much easier to forgive others and yourself in present time.

Desire is like a river that when blocked becomes stale and murky. But by letting go in the freedom of considering infinite possibilities of what is in the river of desire, the stream begins to flow and automatically begins to purify itself. Let your hidden desires come out in the sunshine of your consciousness, and they automatically will become more aligned with your divine nature. You then will experience the peace, joy, confidence, and love that come from feeling your soul desires.

The Power is already Within You

The miraculous healing and success that any person can now experience, comes from developing our own inner ability to create practical miracles. This power is already within everyone. Our bodies and brain are wired to access and express it. All we have to do is awaken it. Life becomes so much easier when you learn to create practical miracles. Jesus, who is famous for demonstrating miracles, said, 'I have not come to answer your questions; instead, I come to show you what you will become'.

He could not teach others this mastery, as they were not ready, but he could inspire them and give them hope. The great teacher and miracle worker Buddha shared the same vision. He said there were certain questions that he could not answer because the people were not yet ready. The best he could do was to teach an appropriate message for the people of his time to help alleviate suffering. Jesus and Buddha knew that you can only teach what the student is ready to hear and understand.

Wanting and Getting

The real challenge in life is not just getting what you want, but continuing to want what you have. Many people have learned how to get what they want, but then they no longer enjoy it. Whatever they get is never enough, they always feel as if they are missing something. They are not happy with themselves, their relationships, their health, or their work. There is always one more thing to disturb their peace of mind.

Personal success is not measured by who you are, how much you possess, what you have accomplished, but by how good you feel about who you are, what you have done, and what you have. Personal success is not just about feeling good or happy, it also involves feeling confident that you can get what you want and motivated to do what it takes.

As you achieve personal success, life ceases to be a struggle. Life's inevitable challenges will become opportunities to make you more powerful. Mastering personal success is learning how to transform negative feelings into positive feelings and negative experiences into lessons learned. It means that when you fall down, you know exactly how to get back up. Mistakes, setbacks, and adjustments are a part of life, an important part of how we learn and grow.

The secret is staying in touch with your inner peace, joy, love and confidence. The expectation for life to be perfect drops away as you discover that what you attract and create in your life is perfect for you.

Money can't buy happiness

Money does not buy happiness or love. The more we think that money is capable of making us happy, the more we give away our power to be happy without it. We are capable of debunking the illusion that the outer world is responsible for how we feel; that outer success has the power to make us happy. In truth, we are fully responsible.

When we get more money, we are happy, because we believe that we are now able to be ourselves. In every case, money makes us happy because we believe that money allows us to be, do, have or experience what we want. We are deficient in our ability to experience that who we are is already happy, loving, peaceful and confident.

Money, recognition, marriage, children, a great job, terrific clothes, winning a lottery, or any other form of outer success is like a magnifying glass that is turned on your inner feelings. If you are already peaceful, you will feel more peaceful. If you are already happy and loving, you will be happier and more loving. If you are already confident, you will be more confident. Likewise, to the degree that you are not happy, the joy, love, confidence, or peace in your life will diminish. If you are not happy first, getting rich will not make you any happier. If you are already happy and you know that you are not dependent on more money to be happy, greater wealth can make you happier.

The secret of getting what you want, and wanting what you have, is first to learn how to be happy, loving, confident, and peaceful, regardless of outer conditioning. By first learning to be happy with what you already have, material success will follow in an appropriate manner according to what you really want in life.

The inherent promise of all external success is an illusion. Initially getting what we want appears to work, but after a short period of happiness we are unhappy once again. Unfortunately, each time we look to outer success for fulfilment, we feel more emptiness inside. Instead of feeling greater joy and peace in our lives, we feel more turmoil and dissatisfaction. Outer success can be a heaven or a hell, depending on the degree of personal success we have already achieved.

Personal success comes from within, and is achieved when you are able not only to be yourself, but also to love yourself. It is feeling confident, happy and powerful in the process of doing what you want to do. It involves not just achieving goals, but feeling grateful and satisfied with what you have after you get it.

Lasting happiness comes from within. Most of the time, when we are unhappy, we are wanting something. We automatically conclude that we are unhappy because we don't have what we want. As you achieve more personal success, you discover that wanting more creates positive and happy feelings like passion, confidence, determination, courage, excitement, enthusiasm, faith, appreciation, gratitude, love. Desire or wanting more is the nature of the soul, mind, heart, and senses. The soul is always willing to be more; the heart is always longing to love more and have more; and the senses are always wanting to enjoy more. If we are true to ourselves, we will always want more.

It is natural to want more in our relationships. It is good to want more success in our work. It is normal to enjoy the pleasures of the senses and to want more. Wanting more is our natural state. There is nothing wrong with desire. Abundance, growth, love, pleasure, and the movement toward more is the nature of life.

Who we are is already happy. Our true nature is already loving, joyful, confident, and peaceful. To find happiness, we must begin an inner journey to recover and remember who we really are. By looking inside ourselves, we will discover that the joy, love, power, and peace we are looking for is already there.

To achieve personal success, to know and experience your true self, to be free or struggle and begin to experience your power to create and attract success in your life, you need:

What's Love Got to do with It?

When you are dissatisfied in life (no inner success) or you are not getting what you want (no outer success), the basic reason is that you are not getting what you need.

Too much of anything good will eventually numb our ability to enjoy it. Instead of wanting more, we will be trying to get away.

Your soul has the power to attract the love it needs. When your heart wants what is not available to you, you are looking in the wrong direction. Most of the time, when you are not getting what you need, it is because you are trying to get everything from one source. When you experience obstacles to getting what you need, change your focus, change your intention, and begin getting the real support that you need. By knowing where to look and how to get there, you will understand that you can always get the love you need.

Love and support from our parents

Love and support from family, friends, and having fun

Love and support from peers and others like us with similar goals

Love and support from ourselves

Love and support from intimate relationships, partnerships, and romance

Loving and supporting someone who is dependent on us

Giving back to our communities

Giving back to the world

The secret to staying in touch with our true selves is to keep filling up our love tanks. As soon as one tank is full, to stay connected, you must begin to fill another tank. If you don't shift your focus from time to time to make sure all your love needs are being satisfied, you become unhappy. If you only look to your partner for love, you will begin to resent that your partner is not giving you enough. Nothing our partners do seems good enough. We mistakenly assume that working on the relationship will make things better. Instead, we need to focus on filling up another love tank.

The symptoms of a full tank: when a tank is filling up, we experience an increase of positive feeling. At those filling-up times, we may think it is our partners who make us happy, but is actually the joy of connecting with our inner selves that makes us happy. Our partner's love and support allows us to get back to ourselves. When someone sees us or treats us with love, we are then better able to connect to who we are. When a love tank is completely full, the symptom is not continuous fulfilment, but often boredom or restlessness and then dissatisfaction. Although we may think we are dissatisfied with out partners, we are actually feeling the collective emptiness of our other tanks. Ironically, the inevitable symptom of fulfilment is the awareness that we are missing something. If you are in a relationship and you are dissatisfied, instead of trying to make the relationship better, you will be more successful by stepping back and filling up another love tank.

When we are low on self-love, we begin expecting too much from our partners. Since we don't love ourselves, we need more from our partners to feel loved. If I believe that I am good enough, there is little you can do to make me feel inadequate. If I believe that I am not good enough, there is little you can do to make me feel any better. If we are not loving ourselves, we cannot let in the love of others. We are the only ones who can fill up our self-love tank. By focusing on loving and supporting ourselves and feeling more autonomous, we will gradually connect once again to our centre. By taking some time for ourselves, time to do what we want, we begin to feel better again.

There is a natural order to the love tanks. As we grow and get the love we need at each stage, we are building a strong foundation for getting the next kind of love. When children do not get the love, understanding, and attention they need, they don't realize or learn the full truth about themselves. They don't fully understand how special they are and as a result feel less lovable. As a result, when situations in life challenge their worthiness, they disconnect from their natural state of inner love, joy, peace, and confidence. They are held back in life, until they learn to fill the empty or partly filled love tanks of the past.

When couples experience tension, the underlying cause is often that they are not loving themselves. Life is always a process of growth and development. When you stop growing, you begin dying.

Healing the Hurt of the Past

If twenty-one is a time of physical maturity, twenty-eight is a time of emotions maturity. If we have denied the unresolved feelings of our past, they begin to come back. Whatever is left unresolved from our past surfaces. We begin to question everything we learned to be true from others. Now is the time to live our lives by our inner guidance. Certainly others can help us in our journey and give us direction, but now we must feel within our hearts what is true and workable for ourselves. What is good for one person may not be exactly right for you.

If the walls in your house began to crack, you would first look to the foundation to correct the problem. If your plants began to turn yellow and die, you wouldn't try painting them to make them look good. Instead, you would water them. In a similar way, most of our problems begin to go away on their own when we start filling up the love tanks. For most difficulties in life, the solution starts with making sure we are filling first love tank. Many of the feelings we experience are really how we felt as children. By taking some time out of our week to fill our past love tanks, we are able to move forward to create the life we want. It is always best to be doing things each week that keep your tanks full. It is not enough to fill them up once.

The first love tank is love and support from our God image. When we are missing it, life tends to be a struggle. We eventually become tired and distressed, because we think we have to do it all ourselves. To fill this first tank, we need to have regular contact with the image of God we carry in our unconscious mind, or with a spiritual relationship in some way with the universe. We need to understand that we are not alone and that there is a higher power assisting us. Meditation is not just religious, it is spiritual. Even if someone is an atheist or is not affiliated with a particular religion, they can satisfy this basic need with regular meditation.

When we miss the love and support from parents, we tend to be held back in life by feelings of doubt, inadequacy, and unworthiness. We experience emotional disturbance and distress in our lives. We may think it is the world or our jobs that create the distress, but it comes from within. The outer world just reflects our inner world.

Many of the beliefs we formed in early childhood continue to hold us back. By changing the beliefs that were formed early in life, you make everything better right away. Regardless of what kind of support you got in childhood, you now have the power to be a parent to yourself and to give yourself everything you need. Professional helpers, counsellors, therapists, can help you fill this second love tank.

The third love tank is love and support from family, friends and fun. If your primary relationship suffers from criticism, blame or boredom, focus on developing and enjoying friendships, having a good time, nurturing old friendships, creating new friends as well. New friends help bring out new parts of who we are. Old friends help us to love and accept ourselves the way we are. Both are needed. Whenever we have difficulty getting what we need, we are looking in the wrong direction. Humour and play are helpful. When you are feeling down, it is very good to see a funny movie. If you really don't want to, sometimes that is exactly what you need. We often resist the things we need, but once we get involved we start feeling better.

We find the peer support love tank in a club or support group of some kind. It is important that you have some interests separate from your partner. This needs to be your own thing that you share with others. Go places, where people group together. Go to the sports, the movie theatre, participate in religious groups, sing and pray together, you will receive an abundance of peer support. Go to concerts. What a blast it is to go to a Rolling Stones concert to bring you back to how you felt as a teenager. Not only there is a group of people who enjoy the music you like, but the music is what you listened to when you were young. The music you loved as a teenager will always be a powerful anchor to bring you back to feeling the energy of your teenage self. You will be awakening that part of who you are, and drawing in benefits from the particular energy of that stage. By awakening the teenager, you will have surges of enthusiasm, vitality, and energy to move ahead in life. If you have any particular challenge that you need to overcome, attend meetings of others who have met similar challenges.

You always come first. You must be in charge of your life. You must begin asking yourself what you want and then go for it. What turns you on? What makes you happy? What is good for you? Go places where you feel comfortable asking for what you want, and saying no to what you don't want. Get away from people in your everyday life, so that you are free to try on new outfits and behave differently. Give yourself the freedom to do things you would never have done. Go somewhere where you will never go again, so if you make a fool of yourself it doesn't matter, because no one knows you and you will not be back. Much of the time, we hold ourselves back because we are concerned about what others will think of us. We want to do things, but we don't, because if we make mistakes we will be reminded of it forever. Also, being around new and different people always brings out some new part of who you are. Whenever you share with someone new and different, a new part of who you are has a chance to surface. To find outer success and be happy, stay in touch with what you want and set your intentions each day. Imagine going into a restaurant and not ordering. The waiter asks what you would like, and you say, 'Whatever you have'. Unless you are just lucky, you will probably get leftovers. Take a few minutes everyday to reflect on what you want, and then set your intention by putting in your order.

Relationships, partnerships, romance

Make sure that you are sharing yourself with someone. You depend on that person and that person depends on you. When the student is ready, the teacher always just appears. When you ask the question, the answer will come. When you are ready for a relationship and you are open to dating, the perfect person for you shows up. If you are desperate, the perfect person rarely shows up. Give up your neediness by having a life that supports your other needs, and you will draw the right partner for you. Soul mates are never perfect, but they are perfect for you as partners. Since there is a deep connection, you are immediately connecting back to your true self by loving them. There are thousands of people with whom you could have a perfect partnership. A soul mate is one of those people you choose to share your life with. To create love and lasting relationships, we need to learn new skills. If we are not actively creating opportunities for romance to thrive, it won't. Not only does romance fulfil our heart's desire for greater intimacy, but it helps empower us to be more successful in the world. All the techniques for creating more in the outer world require that we be in touch with our feelings and desires. If we are suppressing our sexual desires or are numb to them, we are cutting out a tremendous amount of power in our lives. Staying in touch with, and acting to fulfil all our desires, is essential to create and attract everything you want.

Being responsible for the needs of others is an essential requirement of the soul. We cannot continue to develop after age thirty-five if we don't create opportunities to give unconditionally. We must feel responsible to someone else whom we care for and love. We can give unconditionally only when our tanks are full, and we are overflowing. This is the ideal challenge in this time period of development. It is not enough to take care of the poor or a nephew or niece. We need to feel deeply responsible for someone or something alive. If you don't have children, a very good replacement is having a pet or garden to look after. By feeling responsible and giving your love unconditionally, making sacrifices and not asking for something in return, your soul will be strengthened.

Give back to your community, assist in making your local world a better and more beautiful place. Do volunteer work to help others not directly related to you. Schools, library, the environment. The gifts we have received in life are the gifts we have to share with our community. Give time and money to charities and worthy organizations that are trying to help your community. By extending yourself in this way, you begin to expand your spirit through your generosity. Be careful that you don't neglect your family in the process.

We need to broaden our horizons and extend ourselves beyond the boundaries of our community, race, and culture. This is a time to share with those of different backgrounds and traditions. It is a time to become more interested in political ideals and ideas in your community and around the world. You may get involved in politics or in some kind of world cause. This is also an ideal time to travel and see the world and share your light. Take more vacations and broaden your experiences. If you do not expand your boundaries, you will not grow. By connecting and sharing yourself in other cultures, you will discover that, although people are different, we are all the same deep inside. Seeing the world will bring out new parts of who you are, and will keep you young. This is also a time when your business may thrive. When you are full within yourself and capable of giving back to the world, your own success dramatically increases. The more you have done for others, assuming that it is without strings attached, the more power you will have to attract what you want.

Just as you can draw in positive energy, you can send out negative energy. When you have accumulated stress during the day, you can send that negative energy out of your body. De-charging is just as important and easy as meditating and setting your intentions. When people are stuck in any of the blocks to personal success (blame, depression, anxiety, indifference, judgments, indecision, procrastination, perfectionism, resentment, self-pity, confusion, and guilt), they are producing some degree of negative energy. This doesn't mean they are bad or negative, but it does mean they are disconnected from their inner source of positive energy. In the absence of positive energy, they put out negative energy. If they are drawn to you, it is often because you make them feel better. They draw in your positive energy.

You have probably had the experience of going somewhere or being with some people who cause you to start to feel worse. In a similar way, you could be with others and automatically begin to feel better and better. These experiences are the result of an exchange of energy. When one person is low in energy, just being around someone with high energy will give that person a boost. Yet the person with high energy will have a little less. Energy flows from one person to another to find a balance or equilibrium. Although this example describes the flow of energy in quantity, it doesn't describe it in quality. When positive energy flows out, it does not just become less, it will attract and absorb negative energy. If you are feeling good and you connect with someone who is feeling worse, after a while the other person will begin to feel better and you start to feel bad. You may not feel it right away, but within a few hours or days you will begin to notice that your good feelings are missing.

When one person is stuck in negative energy, just being around a person with positive energy will make the person feel better. Gradually the person with positive energy will begin to feel a little less positive. A person who has a lot of positive energy will take a while before noticing that some negative energy has been absorbed. A person whose level of energy is low will notice and be influenced by the negative energy right away.

The more sensitive you are, the more you will notice the different flows of energy and be influenced by them. If you are not sensitive, you will not be so influenced. Your 'valve', to different degrees, is closed. You are well protected, but you are also not able to draw in greater degrees of energy. Some people are just less sensitive. They don't notice this flow of energy at all, and they are not influenced by it. They get their energy from food, exercise, air, sex, and that's it. They are more stable, they get things done, and they can be very successful. They do what others before them have done, and experience different degrees of success or failure largely depending on opportunities, genes, childhood rearing, education, past actions, and the natural talent they were born with. They have not yet tapped their inner creative potential. They can repeat, but they cannot create. To change their destiny, to discover their creative potential, to change their direction in life, they need to become more sensitive.

On the other hand, many people suffer tremendously simply because they have not learned how to release the negative energy they absorb from others. They collect and carry around negative energy. Either they send it back out to others, or they try to be really loving and good, and that negative energy stays stuck in their bodies and creates sickness and disease. Their negative energy gradually weakens the body and blocks the natural healing energy that allows others to get better. Some very loving and positive people get sick because they absorb negativity, but do not send it out. If you are sensitive, unless you find a way to de-charge the negativity you absorb, you will continue to suffer unnecessarily.

By processing emotions and by regular de-charging, you can learn to transform negative feelings. Absorbing negative energy becomes a problem only because we have not learned to de-charge it.

A lifetime of negativity will begin to drain out of you as you practice de-charging.

When you suppress negative emotions, you numb your ability to feel your true desires. If you can't feel sadness, then you can't feel how much you miss someone and want to be with that person. If you can't feel anger, then you can't feel what you don't want. If you can't feel your fears, then you can't feel your needs for love and support. If you can't feel your sorrow, they you have no compassion and life loses its meaning and purpose. All the negative emotions link us back to important aspects of our true selves.

If you suppress your emotions, you do not continue to grow. You don't even know what you're missing. By suppressing your feelings, you find immediate relief, but you stop growing. When we suppress our feelings, when we disconnect from our inner feelings, we disconnect from our inner source of happiness, and we become increasingly dependant on the outer world, and our lives become devoid of passion, creativity and growth.

When people are stuck in any of the blocks to personal success, they are often chronically disconnected from their inner source of positive energy, that is why some people never get better in therapy: they work on feeling better, and as soon as they go back out into the world, they just pick up more negative energy and get stuck. Some people exude negative energy because of their life style, friends, and thinking habits. Being around these people will actually make you sick. To be around other people more in touch with their true nature will actually make you feel better. This is why we are drawn to successful people. The solution to absorbing negative energy is not becoming less sensitive, but learning to de-charge. Recharge through meditation and discharge again. Send out the negative energy where it will do no harm. Negative energy is automatically absorbed and transformed by Nature. This is why if you are stressed you automatically become more relaxed by going for a walk in a forest or garden, or enjoying the beach or lying in the sun. The elements of nature absorb our negativity and send out positive energy. By directing or de-charging our negative energy into nature it is automatically transformed into positive energy once again.

After meditating for a while, lower your hands, point them in the direction of a live plant, fire, water, repeat a meditation phrase over and over with an intention to send your negativity out and into whatever you are pointing at. This is de-charging. When you send your negative energy to an object of nature, it just absorbs all your negativity and you feel better. This is not hurtful to Nature. Nature absorbs and recycles the energy you de-charge.

Nature always seeks a balance. When you have a lot of positive energy, you will attract negative energy. The secret of personal success is to continue to recharge and then de-charge the negativity you absorb. Trying to avoid negativity is only important if you are tired and sick, but if you are recharging every day through meditation, then sharing your love and light with the world is what brings the greatest fulfilment and strength. As you develop your ability to draw in positive energy and de-charge negative energy, confronting the challenges of negativity will make you stronger.

The Importance of Letting Go

There is a big difference between letting go of negative emotions and not feeling them. To let go of them, we have to feel them. Through feeling and releasing negative emotions we are able to fully discharge negative energy. The reason for extraordinary material progress, creativity, and power in the world is more awareness of what we are feeling and what we want. Feeling emotion is pure energy that connects us to God and the world. When emotions are blocked, either we cannot get the energy and love we need, or we are unable to get the power to attract and manifest what we want. To the extent that you dwell on negative emotions you will attract that in your life. To the extent that you deny your emotions you will disconnect with your power to create what you want.

Processing your feelings means identifying your negative emotions and releasing them by getting in touch with your underlying desires and positive feelings. Processing negative emotions is using them to come back to the true self. Balance is achieved by regularly going off centre and then coming back. Wiggling from side to side is the process of sustaining balance. In the beginning, this is very dramatic, and quite often we fail and have to start again. As we get the hang of it, we learn to make adjustments to keep our balance. The only way we can keep balance on a bike, is to notice when we are moving off centre to the left or right. When we move to the left, we need to move back to the right to find balance, and then back to the left, and then back to the right. Likewise in the process of living. When we move off centre to the left, a negative emotion comes up. As we let go of that movement and return to centre, we move the other way, and another negative emotion emerges. Once again, by feeling the next negative emotion, we realise we are moving too far to the right, and we adjust that movement to come back to the centre. With a bike, we don't expect always to be in perfect balance. When it comes to negative emotions, we mistakenly assume that to stay balanced in our centre or true self we should never feel pain or negative emotions. We resist the process, because we don't know how to deal with our negative emotions to find a balance again. As you learn to process your negative emotions, it will become an effortless part of your life. To experience the richness and fullness of life you have to stay in touch with your emotions – all your emotions. Through staying in touch with your feelings you can fully enjoy the richness of life's simple pleasures.

Most of the time, when we are stuck, we may think we are upset with someone, when we really are upset with ourselves, or afraid about something at work. If I am stuck being angry with a business associate, I would ask myself who else or what else I am upset about. Suddenly I may begin to feel that I am upset that I am behind schedule. Once I change the content of my upset, I feel I am on the right track, but the anger is still not releasing. Then I would ask myself what I am sad or disappointed about. As I begin to feel my sadness or disappointment, my anger automatically lessens and I start to become more understanding, my thinking becomes more open and forgiving. Since I'm coming back to the centre, the negativity is almost gone. I feel greater trust that I can find a solution. I begin to appreciate what is working, and release my focus on what is not working. Much of the time what you think you are upset about is just the tip of the iceberg. By getting inside yourself and exploring other things that may be bothering you, you will find that you can give up resisting what you cannot change, and that what you are really upset about can be changed, either by a little shift in your attitude or by a change in your behaviour.

By linking what we are feeling now to events in the past, we can very effectively find a release. When we are angry in present time, it is harder to surrender and let go because we think we have to be angry to get things done. When we are sad in present time and feeling a loss, we are not experiencing that the future will always bring more. When we afraid in present time, we don't know what the future holds, but when we look back and re-experience the fear we felt in the past, we have the added benefit of knowing that things were not as bad as we thought they were, and that things did get better. With the advantage of hindsight, it is much easier to release negativity. Think for a moment about all the times you got really upset about something and later realized that it was not such a big deal. Think about the times when you were afraid of the worst happening and it didn't. Even when the worst has happened to us, things eventually change and get better. Re-living and then enriching the experience, for example by writing the loving response you want in that moment, will help you release your negative emotions.

Whenever you are upset and you don't know why, clearly what you feel has nothing to do with right now. To feel and release the emotions, you have to create a context that can nurture and release the feeling. If you can't find a reason for your feelings, your mind starts to create one. If we can't create a safe context in which to feel and release emotions, we are automatically drawn to or attract situations to validate these unresolved feelings. What keeps us from moving ahead to create the life we want is the tendency to repeat the past; we need to experience the feelings that come up, to fill the earlier love tanks, to look at what is needed to be resolved, or your past will come to you by repeating patterns, and you are drawn again and again to situations that will validate your pain.

When we attract negative situations that are not even close to what our mind is wanting, the soul is drawing in situations to help us get in touch with something, and to release our negativity. The soul knows that sometimes there is no other way to reconnect with our true self, unless a context is created to feel the pain we are suppressing.

Sometimes, rather than looking back to process our feelings, we can look ahead. For a few minutes, imagine that whatever is happening continues to get worse. See everything that you are angry about continuing on. See your biggest fears actually coming to pass. Imagine yourself in the future having that experience, and create a link to your past. By looking directly at your fears, you feel sad, hurt, discouraged. Then link these sad and hurting feelings to a time in the distant past, and begin processing your feelings.

Another way to get unstuck and process your negative emotions is, instead of focusing on your pain, taking some time to focus on the pain of others. When something happens in a movie and tears well up in your eyes, you may not even know why you have such a strong reaction, but clearly it's because of something in your past. A nerve has been touched. There is an added benefit to being in a movie theatre with other people sharing what you feel. Reading books has the same healing influence. By living through another person's pain and joy, we can more fully stay in touch with our own. The reason for drama is that the characters act out the problems we experience in life. Since their circumstances are more tragic or more humorous, it is easier for us to feel with them.

In our own lives, we often suppress our feelings, because our minds invalidate them. When movies, great stories, books, and theatre help to dramatise the pain, we accept the pain and sorrow of characters and we share it; when they resolve, we experience the release. Music and singing also heal the heart through extreme emotions as elation, salvation, hope, devastation, rage, betrayal, despair.

When we heal the pain of others as we give them compassion, our inner pain has a chance to come up and is sometimes automatically released.

Do you Want What you Get?

The secret of personal success is to be true to yourself, and to continue to want more. It is not enough to be happy. You must also grow in your desire for more. When you really want more, you will get it. In some cases, people might like the idea of having more, but they don't go all the way and really want it, they don't give themselves permission to want it. We must want it so much that it hurts when we don't get it, and we must learn how to release and heal that hurt, so that we can experience inner happiness as well.

Many people who have had humble beginnings, have learned how to be happy with less, but continued to want more. Many other people who have become successful, stop producing, creating or attracting success because they lost their touch with their desire for more. Others, after bottoming out and losing it all, quite often make a comeback. By releasing their pain and then re-learning how to be happy with less, they once again create the fertile ground to plant the seeds of desire. Once they lose it all, they accept and appreciate what they have.

When you continue to feel and act on what you want, the universe responds to your will. Passion, belief and desire are power. By taking action to get what you want, you strengthen your belief. The world will not believe in you until you believe. It's not what you do that counts, but what you want, feel and believe. Certainly some action is required to strengthen your belief, which is what attracts success.

When you take the risk, when you make the commitment, when you make the jump into the abyss of the unknown, you are reinforcing your belief in yourself and the possibility of getting what you want. You must learn to access your inner intention.

Doing too much is sometimes the result of not believing in your power to attract and create success. People overgiving and overworking prevent from achieving success, and disconnect with the belief by relying fully on 'doing' to achieve.

Edison described his genius to create as ninety-nine percent perspiration and one percent inspiration. He would try everything, and when his mind gave up, he would let go and finally experience the inspiration of a genius idea.

Whenever we push ourselves to our limit, we feel our limit by experiencing negative emotions. The limit means we can't feel positive about this anymore. When we push to our limit and then let go, we are turning it over to God, spirit, or that mysterious source of brilliant ideas. When we remember that we don't have to do it ourselves, we can relax a lot more; we are not alone, we are helped. When we experience our connection to spirit, by setting our intentions at the beginning of each day, we don't have to do so much. Whatever we do, we are really just telling the mind, body or heart what to do. We don't have to think about it. Turning it over to God means remembering that all you have to do is drive the car, but not pushing it.

Positive thinking does not work when people use it to deny their true feelings and wants, when they tend to suppress their negative emotions. Instead of feeling the pain of not having what they really want, or not getting what they want, they choose to focus on the positive. They need to experience their full power to create, attract and get through wanting.

The Vocabulary of Self-Belief

Go with the flow, accept and forgive, surrender and let God's will be done, give up your desires, be of service, give up your ego, rise above negative emotions, fear and sickness are an illusion, expect a miracle.

Keep your heart open and continue to want what you want. People lose their creative power because they give up and stop believing. The secret of creating is sustaining a strong, wilful intention. 'I will have that, I really want it, and I trust that it will come'. It's desire plus trust.

Whenever you risk doing that which is closer to where you are, the thought of rejection or failure is greater. It is one thing to be rejected by others for the clothes you wear; it is an entirely different story to be rejected for your beliefs. When you are true to who you are, you are exposed; if you are rejected or criticized, it cuts much closer and it hurts more. It pushes your buttons and brings up unresolved issues and feelings from the past. By learning to process the past feelings of abandonment, failure, and powerlessness, you'll be free from anxiety. Fear is greater when we risk being true to ourselves. We need to become very conscious of the ways we may be pushing down or denying our true desires.

Trust, caring and strong desire are the ingredients of power. When you don't get what you want, it's important to let yourself feel deeply disappointed and sad. Yet all this intense feeling doesn't have to rip our lives apart. Women often can feel many of their emotions, but they have hard time trusting and letting go. Men, on the other hand, have had a little easier time letting go and knowing what they want, but it is much harder for them to feel their emotions fully.

By focusing a lot of his energy on what he wants, a man sets the stage for getting in touch with his feelings. By setting goals and really going for it, if things don't always work out, he can feel his loss more deeply. As a result, the power of his desire and belief will increase. Taking reasonable risks and pushing to his limits helps him to feel his emotions.

Taking time to share his feelings with others is not as important for a man. Women can build trust and learn to release their negative emotions, by focusing more on acknowledging the different wants and needs behind their painful emotions. As a woman connects more with her wants, the inherent knowledge and wisdom of how to get them emerges and provides her with greater trust. Taking risks and pushing to her limits is not as important for her, but sharing her emotions in a supportive context assists her greatly in feeling her wants.

As a woman feels her emotions and desires more deeply, she begins to believe, 'I deserve to have more, I deserve to be successful, I deserve greater abundance in my life right now'. As a man is able to connect more with his feelings and wants, he is able to increase his caring. As he is able to 'feel' his desires, the intuitive knowledge that he can get what he wants emerges. His confidence increases and he feels up to the job at hand. By taking time to review his goals and acknowledge his feelings as they come up, he is able to keep his edge. He can continue to stay hungry for more, and motivated to get it.

When your desires are strong, the intuitive knowledge of what is possible comes into focus. It just becomes evident to you. Increasing trust and caring create passion and enhance your power to create what you want. Then, if you just focus your attention on what you want, that desire will begin to manifest in your life. Not only will your thinking be more creative, but things will just go your way.

The secret to increasing your power to get what you want, is to feel your negative emotions when you don't get what you want, and release them. As you learn to release negative feelings, you are left feeling your true desires. By connecting with your true nature, you once again have the power to create what you want and want what you have.

When we don't know how to release our negative emotions, the easiest way to leave them behind is to stop wanting. If not getting something I want bothers me, I simply stop wanting it, or lessen my desire. If I adjust my desire always to accept what I get, I can be free of negative emotions. Some people are very happy doing this, but then wonder why they may be bored, or why they are not getting more of what they want. When we believe in our future, we open the door for more to come in. We must believe and we must ask. If you don't ask, you don't get.

The blessing of free will is the power to will ourselves into hell or heaven, not after we die, but right now. What you desire is what you get. The Universe responds to all desires. It doesn't matter whether you believe in God or not; plenty of people who have made millions or billions don't believe in God. Asking for God's help in achieving outer success just makes the process more fulfilling and less stressful. Like a wise, loving parent, God can only do for you what you can't do for yourself. When children are young, parents do more, and as they get older, parents let them do more, so that they can gain confidence and independence. God always gives us the opportunity to do all that we can do. That is how we grow in confidence and faith, and miracles happen most.

Whenever some disappointment or setback happens, things are constantly adjusted so that events can happen when they are supposed to. When you regularly set your intentions, what might seem like chance is the direct result of setting those intentions, and letting your intention guide you to getting exactly what you want. The secret is to start small. Always throw in a few extra things, just to open the door for more to come in. When things happen, you realize your power to create the day the way you want. Life is a series of little miracles, and occasionally some real big ones start happening: things get organized in a way that you could never orchestrate yourself; people change overnight in the way they deal with you.

Giving up Resistance

Why is it that when we don't want something, it tends to follow us through life? Quite often what we resist persists. We think that by resisting what we don't want it will go away. Well, it won't. It is by giving up our resistance that we are free to create what we want. When we resist what we don't want, we just add power to someone or a situation, we are giving it full attention. At work, the people we resist the most are somehow the ones we are forced to deal with on a regular basis. Actively focusing on what we don't want weakens our power. We unknowingly waste our energy. Our thinking is far more powerful than most people understand. Ninety per cent of what gets done in life is caused by thinking, while ten per cent is action. What you put your attention on in life just increases. The more we have healed our past, the less we are affected by its ghosts. Unless we can let go of the pain associated with a past event, we tend to get stuck in a negative pattern of repeating certain aspects of it.

Our negative comments reflect a world of resistance within. Start by being aware of what you say, that what you say is what happens. The power of your words is enormous, particularly when you express a true desire. Rephrase your negative thoughts: instead of saying 'my partner never helps me anymore' say 'I want my partner to offer help out'. The secret to asking for more is do it without conveying a message of blame, shame or guilt. Each time ask again as if it was the first time: in the office, at school, at home.

Taking time to remember your positive experience is essential for building confidence and belief. When we feel emotional pain, we are in some way experiencing a negative an untrue belief. Pain is always caused by believing what is not true. When we feel pain, the mind believes something, and the soul is saying it is not true. To change the belief, we have to get back to feeling the pain, and our mature mind reconnects and self-corrects.

Recognising and Honouring Desires

When you are not experiencing inner success, you are not in touch with your soul's desire. When you are not experiencing outer success, you are not connecting with your mind's desire. When you are not attracting what you need, you are not fulfilling your heart's desire. When you are not healthy or vibrant in your body, you are not fulfilling your body's desires.

Since we have different kinds of desires, sometimes they conflict as well. The mind wants things to make us powerful, while the soul wants to be loving and happy. When we cannot see the whole picture, the mind may want money right away, and not care about being happy or loving in the process. In Western materialistic circles, the mind dominates the soul and wins the battle. In the Eastern traditions, the soul tends to win the battle. The mind wants to be happy and believes that happiness can only come from within, so it honours the soul's desire, but suppresses its own passionate desires for outer success. Soul, mind, heart and body desires are all different but can coexist and work together.

Revenge… not so sweet

By learning to release blame with forgiveness, you will be free of this tendency to waste your energy and power trying to get even. As long as you are holding to the desire to punish, get even, or teach someone a lesson, you will just be giving them space in your brain free of charge. The energy, time and attention you have to make your dreams come true gets wasted on them. When you let go of revenge, you take back your power to be happy and fulfilled within yourself without depending on the outside.

Attachment

When we lose someone or something, we feel sadness, fear, sorrow, frustration. If you don't let go you will continue to want what you can't have anymore, you will push away your glorious future. The secret of continuing to love is to let go when it is time to change. When we are used to getting love and support from someone, when we lose access to that support, we disconnect from our inner selves. To feel loving, we think we need that person and do not yet realize that we really need the love and support that person provides us. The support to reconnect with ourselves can be found elsewhere. There are always other ways to fill up our love tanks. Temporarily, we will suffer from our emptiness. As you learn to fill your love tank through prayer and meditation, you will experience a lift in your spirit. When you can directly taste the happiness you thought only the new TV would bring, you are no longer so attached. You still want the TV, but not because you have to have it to be happy. You want it, but you are not attached. This holds a lot of power.

Doubt your Doubts

To access your creative power to solve problems and create what you want, you have to start from uncertainty. There is a big difference between doubt, which is not believing, and simply not knowing. From a place of not knowing, you can still believe that something is possible. When you are stuck not believing, when you really are just uncertain, then doubt your doubts, and look at what could be possible. If you already know something, you are not open for more. But when there is a question, the answer will come. When the need exists, the solution is always nearby. The challenge with uncertainty is to keep asking for answers. Whenever you do not know what to do next, ask 'show me the way' and eventually the insight comes and you get what you want.

Whenever you feel anxiety, you can release it by reminding yourself that you have started to doubt, instead of accepting that you just don't know.

Uncertainty always precedes getting an answer, a clearer insight. To let go of anxiety, ask yourself what you are afraid of. Then ask yourself if you know for sure that those things will happen. Most anxiety is believing our fear, instead of remembering that we really do not know. By opening your mind to all possibilities, you can begin to tap into your inner guidance and to feel trust.

Doubt kills passion and stops the flow of feeling. When people say and feel what they want, they are automatically connecting with the part of them that knows or believes that they can have what they want. Letting go of doubt allows you to focus on what you want, rather than waste your power resisting what you do not want. Natural healing energy becomes blocked because some part is missing faith and doubting, so a current of energy cannot flow into a person to heal them.

Another way we block our true desires is by rationalizing away our true desire. Even when our heart says we do not want to do something, the mind dominates by explaining why it must be done. We may say 'this is my job' or 'these were my orders'. People mindlessly do things that are against what they feel, by rationalizing their feelings. Rationalization also occurs when we do not believe we can do something or we think it is not possible for us. We rationalize our desire by saying to ourselves, 'Do not be upset', 'You can't win them all', 'It's just not your thing', 'Your goals were unrealistic', 'It's not yet possible', 'It's not the right time'.

Self-talk is very helpful as long as we first get a chance to feel, and then release our emotions. We conclude that to let go of negative emotions, we have to talk ourselves out of them, which in fact will either increase or suppress them, along with our ability to feel what we want. The time spent becoming aware of, and then feeling, negative emotions, is enough to release them. Children will return automatically to positive feelings if able to feel freely and share their negative emotions with a loving and understanding listener. As adults, we are not so dependent on others to help us release our negative emotions. After about age twenty-one, we can begin to exercise our potential to listen to ourselves with love and understanding. That is good, since other adults generally do not want to hear negative emotions. As adults, if we just take time to write down our thoughts, feelings, and desires, we can listen to what is going on inside. If we learn to listen without judgment or resistance, the negative emotions will head us right back to our true positive self.

As soon as we rationalize or try to walk away our negativity, we will cause suppression and disconnection from our true nature. Rationalization may work temporarily to create relief, but it is counterproductive. Besides disconnecting us from our true selves, it drains us of life force and results in sickness, boredom and lifelessness. Suppressing emotions takes away energy. Even more important, rationalizing can cover up our feelings of remorse that allows us to self-correct. We may do something that hurts others, but by rationalizing we deny our soul's desire to be compassionate: 'There was no other way to get what I needed', 'I shouldn't feel bad, I wasn't responsible'. With this denial, we disconnect from our compassionate selves. Even when we are not responsible for a loss or tragedy, it is natural to feel sorrow and wish that it could have been different. These kinds of cold rationalizations harden the heart, and prevent us from connecting to the world. Quite often we will do things though our hearts will say 'no'. Our minds come in and create reasons that we should not follow our hearts, but natural feelings of sorrow are the doorway to conscience. One of the greatest sources of energy and motivation is feeling compassionate for others. It awakens your true desire to be of service and make a difference.

Sometimes, when someone really annoys us, we will want to defy that person, or rebel against what that person wants us to do. We refuse to do something, not because we do not want to, but because a certain person wants us to do it. We may get great satisfaction from doing the opposite of what the person wants, but we will have leaked our power. We think we are 'showing them', but all we are showing is that the person is still controlling us. We are the ones who lose, when we do not do what we want. All power comes from doing what you want. When we change ourselves because of someone else's bad manners, we are the ones who lose. There is so much energy wasted in lawsuits. Rather than waste money, time, energy, and focus on a lawsuit, move on and create what you want.

Surrender and Submission

Submission is stop believing in ourselves and give up our desire.

Surrender is giving up our resistance to what is, it is not stop wanting what we want. Surrender is adjusting our expectations of how soon we will get what we want, it frees us from demanding what we need in a particular wrapping. Surrender nurtures patience but does not preclude persistence and strength. We may have to surrender the expectation that our parents will ever love us the way we want, but we do not have to stop wanting to receive pure, unconditional love. Surrender frees us and opens us up to receive what we want in a variety of different ways. Who cares who gives us what we need, as long as we get it? Remember the serenity prayer: 'God, grant me the serenity to accept the things I cannot change, the courage to change the things I can, and the wisdom to know the difference'.

Avoidance

Often, when we feel helpless to get what we need and want, we will replace our wants with secondary wants, replacement desires. Often we are afraid of failure so we put things off. We could spend much of our lives going in the wrong direction when we just need to make a few adjustments, and take a few steps in the right direction, and everything will start to work out. Quite often, when we are looking for a partner, we are really seeking to avoid our feelings of loneliness. When we hunger for success, we are sometimes running away from feelings of failure and inadequacy that still need to be healed. When we are tired or want to take a nap, sometimes we are running away from feeling responsible for something. Our desires for more may be an attempt to avoid our inner feelings. People may feel stressed at work and dream of another job, when what they really want is to be happy at work, to have a job that they enjoy and feel challenged by, to be doing something purposefully each day. When we run away from our problems, they will be waiting wherever we go. So much energy is wasted when we procrastinate. One technique to overcome procrastination is to keep visualizing doing what you are procrastinating. As soon as you shift from feeling what you do not want to what you do want, you realize a tremendous creative power.

Defend Against your Defenses

Some people lose touch with what they truly want by over-defending or justifying their position. Rather than make up after an argument by looking at how they contributed to the problem, they refuse to acknowledge their contribution until the other person apologizes first. By making their feelings of regret and responsibility depend on whether they get an apology, they disconnect with their inner desire to learn from everything and grow.

There are always good reasons to explain why one makes a mistake, but a mistake is still a mistake. If we do not acknowledge our mistakes, we cannot fully connect to our inner feelings of regret, sorrow and remorse, and it is almost impossible to self-correct our attitudes and behaviours. By becoming aware of your tendencies to defend and how they hurt you, you can appropriately defend yourself from your defenses. Defensive tendencies emerge because we are afraid of being punished for our mistakes. When we excuse ourselves by saying we did not know better, we suppress our desire to be more attentive and caring; rather we need to forgive ourselves and trust that others will forgive us as well.

Reject Rejection

When children are deprived of touch, often the result is that later in life they do not feel comfortable being touched. If we are deprived of an important need while growing up, we stop feeling the need, and later in life if someone tries to give us what we need, we will reject it. Our soul keeps drawing into our life the love and support to us, but we are not interested. To break this tendency to reject what we really want and need, we must ask someone we trust to give us what we know we need but feel uncomfortable receiving, so we give ourselves permission to resist and explore and process all the feelings that come up. When you are able to experience and release the negative feelings linked to your rejection, you will begin to appreciate receiving what you need. That appreciation then becomes a magnet to attract more. One of the symptoms of rejecting what you need is the formation of an opposite desire. You will want others, who cannot give you what you need, to give it to you. Quite often we reject the people who have what we need. We long to be loved by, or to work with, people who do not have what we need. By rejecting what we really need, we attract or create situations that mirror unresolved conditions of our childhood.

Jealousy is a very important emotion to bring us back to feeling what we really want and need. It's not bad to be envious of the very rich, because by letting yourself feel the jealousy and feel your desire, you increase your power to get what you want. Unless you feel your earnest desire, you cannot create the abundance that you really want. Whenever you are envious, say 'That's for me'. A positive sign that you are on your way to having what you want is being happy for the success of others and wishing to have it, too.

Withholding only Holds you Back

One of the biggest blocks to getting in touch with your true desire to love and be loved is withholding love. When people hurt us, often our reaction is to withhold our love. Our motivation is either to punish or to protect ourselves from being hurt again. Either way, we are the ones who suffer, because we suppress and deny our heart's desire, we disconnect from our true selves. We cannot fully thrive in life, until we learn to forgive and love again, when our hearts are closed or we withhold the love we feel. If we have been hurt by someone, we need to make an adjustment so that we do not get hurt again. We do not have to stop being loving. To love someone does not mean that we have to please that person, or do what that person wants. It does not mean we have to do anything. It just means our hearts are open to that person. We can see the good in that person and wish that person well. When there is a tendency to withhold, the best way to release it is to vent. To vent, write out all your feelings about the person or situation. Sometimes this procedure involves spending more energy on someone who is not willing to make up with you, but at least you can forgive and wish the person a good life.

Respond Rather than React

When we mindlessly react, we let others determine what we are willing to do. Being generous is one of our soul's desires. If we are really willing to accommodate and help someone, we can't let that person's manners keep us from being true to ourselves.

Many sincere people, who are trying to help the world or do their best at work, become jaded by criticism. They stop wanting to help, because their efforts are not being appreciated. As a result, they gradually lose their power. To be powerful, we have to be able to overcome these challenges, and not let them keep us from feeling and doing what we really want to do. To keep your powers, do not let others and their lack of manners or respect bring you down their level. You sustain your grace, power and position by not matching their energy and sending it back. Instead of reacting, you are choosing how you want to treat them. When someone gets angry with us, we automatically become angry back. This is a reaction. When you send anger back out, others react to you with anger and negativity again. In this way, it goes on. You have to stop the endless cycle of reactions. Our soul's desire is never to hurt someone. Most of the time, when we are experiencing negative emotions, it is best to keep them to ourselves, rather than taking it on others.

The Twelve Negative Emotions

There are twelve basically pure negative emotions: anger, sadness, fear, sorrow, frustration, disappointment, worry, embarrassment, jealousy, hurt, panic, and shame. All other emotions stem from those basic twelve. Feeling a few of these negative emotions will allow us to come back to our true selves, and remove the emotional blocks we may be having. The negative emotions let us know when we are off balance. They help us to remember what we really want. When we come back into balance and connect with our true selves the negative emotion just goes away and we are left with positive feeling. Negative emotions let us know when we are off balance, but the blocks reveal that we have fallen over.

Let Go of the Twelve Angry Blocks

The usual blocks to progress and development in life are blame, depression, anxiety, indifference, judgment, indecision, procrastination, perfectionism, resentment, self-pity, confusion, and guilt.

Blame

When you blame others for your lack of happiness, you give up your ability to heal yourself from sickness and unhappiness. Blame prevents you from taking responsibility for your life, and affirms that you are powerless. As long as someone else is responsible for how you feel, you forfeit the power to change your life. We need to determine the cause of our pain; once we have determined who and what caused our pain, we need to release the blame. If you stole my money from me and it hurt my business, blame is helpful to recognise what happened, and I can correct it and avoid it happening again. If I continue to blame you for my lack of success, I am holding on to the belief that I cannot create what I want because of you. This limited belief prevents me from being able to create my future. I have put you in charge.

When we are in a blame mentality, this fact is hard to comprehend. It is easier if we shift out of this mentality for a moment. Imagine that you have achieved complete personal success. You have complete confidence that you always have everything you need available to you and you have realised your ability to get what you want. You know from experience that what you think and believe are what you get. You trust that you are in the process of getting everything you want. You know that ninety percent of what makes something happen, is being your true loving self, and passionately desiring what you want. With this positive attitude of personal success, there is no reason or need to hold on to blaming others.

If you have a hundred thousand dollars, and someone steals you five dollars, it is OK to feel and release your negative emotions, but it is not healthy to hold on to blame. We need to move on and bless that person. Forgiveness is letting go of the tendency to hold others responsible for our plight in this world. You may feel 'If I forgive you, you will just do that to me again'. When hurt, some people want to punish or withhold love. The only person revenge really hurts is you. Letting go of the blame and finding forgiveness does not mean that you will treat the person the same. If someone hurts you, forgiveness means letting go of the hurt; it doesn't mean that we should in any way allow that person to hurt us again. All people make mistakes but they are still worthy of love. Forgiveness allows you to come back to your loving nature, but alerts you to choose how you want to relate with this person in the future. To forgive does not in any way obligate you to do anything for the person, nor is the person obligated to you.

Whenever you're not getting what you need, you are looking in the wrong direction. When you are getting what you need and filling up a love tank, letting go of blame is almost automatic. The negative belief associated with blame is: 'Because of what happened I can't get what I need or want'. Instead of believing our past holds us back, we recognise that our past can serve us to find our way more clearly and strengthen our ability to love through forgiveness.

Depression

You become depressed when you have disconnected from your innate ability to recognise, appreciate, and enjoy the many blessings in your life. The major cause of depression in women is feeling isolated, or the feeling that she cannot get what she needs. Symptoms of depression are emptiness, or powerlessness. The practice of meditation will bring an immediate lift out of depression. The major cause of depression in men is feeling unneeded. When a man is out of work, or he does not feel appreciated in the office or in a relationship, he will become depressed. He will experience an immediate drop in his energy level, and he will start to feel his life is flat. Symptoms are a lack of motivation and a general feeling that nothing will make a difference, no matter what they do. We need to look in another direction to get what we need or to make a difference.

The negative belief associated with depression is that the love and support you need are not available to you. The new insight is that whenever you feel you can't get what you need, you are looking in the wrong direction, so you have to choose among the hundreds of alternative ways available to achieve your goal. Don't think there is only one way to get what we need or achieve what we want. When we are depressed, we are always expecting life to look a certain way, and it does not. Being attached to the form prevents us from experiencing our success. When we let go of being attached to how something should look, we are then free to attract everything we need and want. One easy way to let go of attachment is first to imagine getting what we need or want. Then imagine how that would make you feel. Relish those feelings. Realise what you really want is to feel that way. Then suppose that there are other ways to have that feeling. This attitude will open your mind and heart to attract what is possible.

Anxiety

You experience anxiety when you have disconnected with your innate ability to trust that everything will work out and always does. When we have not healed certain events in our past, we experience anxiety in the present. It is almost always related to pain in our past that is still unresolved. Problem is that is you do not take risks, and you cannot grow. You deny your inner desires for more, and limit your power. John Lennon said in an interview that he had stopped touring because he would become so nervous that he would vomit before each performance. There are millions of very competent and skilled professionals who still experience nervousness or anxiety. Anxiety in no way is a reflection of actual competence or events to come.

Indifference

When you become indifferent, you have disconnected with your innate ability to know what is possible and what you want. You forfeit your natural motivation and power to change circumstances. Life loses meaning and purpose and becomes devoid of love. Numbness sets in. You feel powerless and deny your true feelings and wants, and thereby lose access to your intuitive knowledge of how to get what you want. Indifference is an automatic response to feeling powerless. Quite often a man's first reaction will be just to shutdown and stop caring. Without passion, he has no power or direction. To avoid the pain, he feels stuck in indifference and not caring. With his heart closed, his life becomes a series of obligations and duties. When a woman begins to believe that she can't get what she needs, her first reaction tends to be mistrust. She has been hurt by depending on others or circumstances and she is not going to be hurt again. By protecting herself, she remains safer, but she cannot grow in love and compassion for herself and others. She becomes cold, mistrusting and detached.

No matter how bad things get, we can always process our negative emotions and come back to feeling much better. Even if the outer situation can't change, we can feel better. After we take this step, outer circumstances always change for the better.

Judgment

You become judgmental when you disconnect from your ability to see the good in others and circumstances. You feel annoyed and irritated by situations that you cannot change, and overlook and miss the positive. While we may be frustrated with the person next to us, we are really worried and even embarrassed about something else. If you are worried about a particular investment or business decision, you may instead feel that worry about something else, and start feeling judgmental about your weight or your partner's. All you notice is 'fat'.

Whenever we fixate on something we can't change, there is always something else that is bothering us. Many times, when we judge others, we are judging ourselves, we are looking in a mirror and not liking what we see. To market yourself, you have to let people know who you are and what you can do. You have to have confidence and put yourself out there without an attitude of 'I am better than you'. Instead, the attitude is more like: 'Look at what I have done, you can trust me'. Many people who do not have a lot of money judge people with money. Some even judge money itself. Either of these attitudes blocks them from receiving money in their lives.

Indecision

You become stuck in indecision, when you disconnect from your inner ability and strength to find your direction and persist; when you lose touch with your inner guidance; when you become too dependent on others to make up your mind. When affected by indecision, you do not develop your inner power to make things happen by the power of giving your word or making a promise.

The major cause of indecision is discouragement and disappointment. When we are facing some of life's more difficult challenges, it is hard to make a decision and move forward. This often occurs because we have not successfully faced and dealt with setbacks, pain regarding mistakes or betrayals in our past. If we have trusted others and they have let us down, it becomes difficult to make a decision to trust others. This tendency sabotages success enormously. To avoid the possibility of failure, we choose to hold back.

To deal with a negative crowd, comedians will remind themselves that any show is rehearsal until you get on the 'Tonight Show'. You do not know if something will work until you try. Gradually you know what works, and then you get a call from the 'Tonight Show'. You don't care if everybody likes you, or what you have to say. You follow your heart and learn from the feedback what works and what does not.

To be successful in the outer world requires making many decisions. Unless you can be comfortable making mistakes, it is very difficult. Besides accepting your mistakes, the next step is realising that you do not have to figure everything out. If you have to make many decisions, first hear them, think about what you want to do, and forget it for a few days. Somehow it goes into the cosmic computer or intuition, and the answer comes out. Unless we make decisions and go for it, we cannot grow and learn.

The mistakes you make today may eventually lead to a solution down the road. It is foolish to think that we can figure out what to do all the time. Life is full of surprises. We need to put in the request and see how we feel a few days later. If, however, you clearly do not know what to do, the best idea is not to do anything. Meanwhile, you process all your feelings, release the stress around the difficult decision, and the answer becomes obvious to you. Some people make the mistake of waiting until they are absolutely assured. This will slow you down tremendously.

Some people are indecisive because they are afraid of disappointing others. This often stems from past experience of not being able to please a parent, or from the fear of making a mistake and losing approval once it had been gained. Making a decision means you know that your decision is the best you can come up with, and you are prepared to deal with the consequences. When you live by your word, you word is stronger. When you always keep your promises, simply by giving your word you will draw in the power to manifest your word.

Procrastination

When you procrastinate, you disconnect from your innate ability to accomplish what you have decided to do. You are unable to get started until you have no choice. You put off or postpone action because you believe that you are not ready or prepared. You forfeit your ability to overcome life's challenges.

Procrastination occurs when courage is weak. Courage is like a muscle. It cannot grow unless you face a challenge and then push into it. If you do not move, the energy that can help you to do what you have to do cannot begin to flow. Nothing can get done if you do not begin. You cannot realise your inner powers if you do not exercise them. Courage grows by taking risks. When you postpone action, you not only suppress your inner powers, gifts and talents, but you suffer. The two greatest causes of suffering in life are not loving, and not doing what you want to do.

We procrastinate when we are worried about something. We generally feel helpless to do what we have said we are going to do. No matter what, we can't seem to do it. To break through this block, we need to realise that the answer lies in changing our feelings. By turning inside and exploring your inner feelings, you will be able to release the negative emotions and feel what you want. When you can fully feel your inner passion, procrastination goes away. By getting out of your head and coming from your passion, you can break through. The pain of failure you seek to avoid, is always much less than the pain of not being true to yourself.

Rather than pushing yourself into action, after each meditation, just keep visualising yourself doing what you want to do. Imagine having the good feelings of relief and accomplishment. Through this process, you will experience the amazing organising power of setting your intentions. In a few days, you realise that you are doing what you wanted to be doing. Another reason some people put off going for what is important to them, is that they believe they are not ready. They believe that if they were ready, they would have no fears, worries, and anxieties. This is not true. No matter how ready you are, you will always have fears. Your fears diminish and go away as you begin. If you wait for them to go away, you will never get started.

Perfectionism

When you disconnect from your innate ability to accept that life is not, and can never be, perfect, you got stuck in the desire to be perfect. As a result, you expect too much from yourself or others. You are never happy or content. You are too demanding. Everything is measured and compared. When nothing is good enough, you cannot freely give and receive love. The need to be perfect begins during childhood when we try to be perfect for our parents, believing that we must be perfect to make our parents happy. Every child is born with the health, desire and longing to please parents. When children are unable to succeed in pleasing their parents, the need to please turns into the need to be perfect. As children, we are so happy when parents are happy with us, and we are so sad when we have disappointed them. To please them, we begin trying to adjust and correct ourselves in ways that deny who we are. As children, we commonly experience upsets at the most inconvenient times. We do not get the positive message that our feelings are OK. A child needs the freedom to feel and experience all the different levels of emotions, and then gradually learn to manage them. If a parent does not approve of a particular emotion, then for sure the child will feel inadequate in some way for feeling that emotion. To win the parents' approval, they seek to suppress their feelings. As children, we are supposed to make many mistakes, to learn our lessons, but often we get the message that if we make mistakes something is wrong with us, we do not get the positive message that it is okay to make mistakes, and we are well on the way to feeling that we have to be perfect.

If we happen to be gifted or talented in some special way, this can also lead to perfectionism, we get special attention for being outstanding. We become accustomed to feeling this praise for being so good. This makes it more difficult for us to risk doing things that we are not so good at. Although perfectionists may be the most accomplished in their fields, they are rarely good enough for themselves. Rather than love what they have created, perfectionists sometimes don't like their work at all.

To get a sense of the underlying feeling of inadequacy that determines many of your surface feelings and desires, make a recording of your voice in conversation. After hearing their voices, most people become very embarrassed and don't like it. Sometimes they can't even believe that is how they sound. The reason this is such a powerful experience is that we have tremendous defences inside to compensate for childhood feelings of inadequacy. We have built up an image of who we are in resistance to negative messages we may have received at different stages. To hear ourselves, because we sound different, brings up our early fears that we are not good enough and that we will be rejected. We feel tremendously embarrassed. It is hard to accept ourselves even through others who are listening think we sound wonderful. If there are negative feelings lurking inside, listening to the recording will immediately bring them up, it can be a trigger to bringing up these feelings, and then you have the opportunity to go back in time to process them.

When we are not feeling perfection in our lives because we are not spiritually connected, we look for that perfection in the outer world. When we connect with our God image, we connect with more, we do not feel we have to be more, do more, or have more to be satisfied. When we want what we have, we can feel our healthy desire to be, do and have more without having to be perfect. This desire for perfection is only unhealthy when we look to ourselves to be perfect in the outer world. When we look inside for perfection, we are trying to discover more of our potential, and that is healthy.

Resentment

You become resentful when you disconnect from your ability to give your love and support. In most cases, you feel you have given more and not received what you deserve in return. You withhold your love because something happened that is not fair. We can only receive love when our hearts are open.

Sometimes we are so resentful that we secretly will not let others give to us. Our hidden message is: 'You are too late. Nothing can make me happy now'. Since we tend to focus on what we did not get with resentment, we miss other opportunities to give and receive. By not forgiving, you continue to live in the past.

Resentment is just another form of blame and judgment. It is a clear sign that you have been giving too much in the wrong direction. Recognise your responsibility for giving too much, and you'll be free to accept the problem without pointing fingers. It will also help to release any guilt.

To break the lock resentment puts on our hearts, we must recognise that we are doing it to ourselves. If you find yourself withholding love, realise that you are creating the problem. When you resent you are now the problem. You not only send out negative energy to others, but that is what you will attract to yourself.

Self-Pity

You have disconnected from your innate ability to appreciate and give thanks for the blessings and successes in your life. When you focus on what you are missing, you lose touch with your ability to appreciate what you have, and do not recognise that many opportunities are available to you.

The cause of self-pity is often lack of attention. A child who is deprived of attention will often seek to get any kind of attention. Though every child needs to be heard and receive empathy, some children have a greater need than the parents can satisfy. As a result, these children learn to paint a bigger and more dramatic problem to get attention. By connecting with the source of fulfilment within, you do not have to get lost in the outer world, hungering for what is already inside.

With self-pity, we not only miss opportunities for more, but we reject them as well. We feel sorry for ourselves, and we do not want anything to change that. We also miss the opportunity to help ourselves. We expect someone out there to make up for what we are missing and make us happy. The tendency to self-pity is released when you are able to feel your anger with others who have rejected and excluded you, and then forgive them.

Confusion

You have disconnected from your innate ability to see clearly, understand, or make sense of what life presents you. Every positive or negative experience has the potential to teach you something useful that you didn't know before.

In confusion, we assume that something important is missing. Instead of being open to finding the answer, we think that we have to have it now. When we think something is missing, we focus on feeling like a victim of circumstances. It is then easy to panic and assume the worst. By looking for and expecting clear and definite answers right away, we miss the bigger picture that life is an unfolding process of learning to be all that we can be.

Life will always present us with challenges and changes that will push us to our limit to understand. Particularly when bad or tragic things happen or seem to be happening, we do not understand why they are happening to us. Without a clear understanding that life presents challenges and obstacles to 'good' people as well as 'bad' people, we begin to think we are bad. We often stay confused to avoid feeling bad or responsible in some way. We cannot understand what good could come from bad or painful things. When setbacks occur, and I do not know why or what to do, I am much more assured that something good will come of it. Everything always works out, often in ways that are far better than we could ever imagine. Take some time to reflect on the many times when you thought things were really urgent or something terrible was going to happen and it did not. So much positive energy is wasted feeling confused rather than trusting that things will work out.

Once you have begun to grow from life's challenges, you understand how they have helped to mould you into what you have become. Imagine that you have achieved all your goals. As you feel grateful for the support you have received, go back and appreciate all the challenges that made you grow and become stronger. As you cultivate an attitude of gratitude for all the lessons learned from life's challenges, you will become free of confusion and experience great wisdom. You cannot stop the world from upsetting you at times, but you can learn to use every setback, upset or negative experience to strengthen and empower you, to discover your inner gifts and powers. Like with muscles in the gym, to grow in personal success you need to be challenged. As you meet each challenge you grow in your abilities.

In life, we think our challenge is to change the outer world. We think the enemy is on the outside.

Our true battlefield is within ourselves. This important recognition frees you to shift your focus from what is wrong to what you can learn.

Guilt

You have disconnected from your innate ability to love yourself and forgive your mistakes. Feeling different degrees of shame after making a mistake is a good thing, but it is not good when the shame does not go away after you recognise and learn from your mistake. Instead of knowing and acting from what you want, you act too much for others, you accommodate too much, and you do not feel comfortable asking for or asserting your wants and needs. You care too much about what others think about you. You forfeit your self-esteem each time you deny your needs to please others.

Being stuck in guilt keeps us from loving ourselves. Either we turn off our feelings because it is too painful, or the guilt eats us day by day. If we are guilty, we have to feel guilty as a first step, next we forgive ourselves and try to make amends if possible. The reason many criminals go back out and commit more crimes is that they have not learned to feel and release their guilt. Rather than feel the pain of their shame for making a mistake, they suppress their feelings altogether and disconnect from their inner conscience, which knows the difference between good and bad, right and wrong. Without a connection to their inner feelings, they justify future crimes by the suffering they had to endure in prison.

To achieve success in life, we must feel self-love and worthy. If we feel unworthy, as soon as we begin to feel our true wants, we begin to suppress them with the belief that we are not deserving. We tend to sacrifice too much for the people we care about, and do not think enough about ourselves. Self-forgiveness is the recognition that we are still innocent deep inside; innocence is a part of who we truly are, and the place we come back to when we release shame.

NEW ENDS, OLD BEGINNINGS

Thank you for having accompanied me in this journey of self-questioning and personal development. If I have shaken (a bit) the foundations of your system of beliefs, I can consider myself privileged and honoured. But, there's a bit more, still.

I'm going to invite you now to a personal incursion into the spiritual/religious/mystical/psychic underworld (whatever name suits you best). I hope that you choose to join in this journey, and heed the call of the essential, the living blocks of humanity, that which differentiates us from beasts, androids or demons.

HAPPINESS

Everyone is interested in being happy; in fact it's one of the few ambitions which is universal to our species.

We are constantly encouraged to believe that we have to achieve, acquire or consume to be happy. But that is far from being the full story.

Living happily depends mainly on your inner life, the conscious world of your thoughts, emotions, beliefs, desires etc. It's a matter of inner peace, peace of mind, peace in the heart. But your inner life in turn is largely based on patterns or habits, the ways you react to what goes on around you. So your happiness depends on these habits. You can't always control what happens in the world around you. You can't even control how you react inwardly to what happens - your inner habits dictate your reaction.

But you are not powerless. If you learn to pay attention to your inner life, you can over time shape the way your inner habits work. By training and changing these habits, you can live with more serenity and peace of mind.

SPIRITUALITY

Spirituality is the sense of feeling connected to everything around us and finding inner peace. Some of the most enlightened and spiritual figures, such as the Dalai Lama, or the Buddha, develop inner peace, kindness, and wisdom through daily practice, and then share their experience with others. They try to not harm others, and to live peacefully and gently, working towards the ultimate goal of pure and lasting happiness for all living beings.

Life is a window of time and an opportunity for us to do meaningful things and find a purpose. It is up to ourselves to find our own purpose and meaning in life; such things are not predetermined by someone or something else. As long as there are problems to be solved, hunger to lessen, illness to cure, pain to minimize, or oppression to resist, there is meaning in life. As long as there are goals to reach, knowledge to gain, beauty to create and appreciate, places to explore, love or dreams to seek after, there is meaning in life. If you want meaning in your life, then do something meaningful.

Many people with so much materially, feel life lacks meaning and purpose. So many feel at a loss, when trying to impart meaning and values to their children growing up immersed in a culture that "knows the price of everything and the value of nothing". So many people feel helpless and frustrated when they read the daily newspaper, or tune into TV current affairs.

And so many have lives totally at odds with their needs as human beings, causing illness, anguish, conflict, frustration, and feelings of loneliness and alienation, from others and even from life itself.

You may wonder how to feel optimistic and contented with life, when there's so much unhappiness and tragedy in the world, when there are so few answers and reasons for excruciating pain. What contribution can a spiritual approach make?

Regardless of how you choose to interpret spirituality, a spiritual life gives you the contentment and freedom that comes with humility, the feeling of belonging that comes from accepting responsibility and knowing right from wrong, and the energy to wake each day and embrace life.

Religions connect humans with a divine presence or numinous force. They bond human communities and they assist in forging intimate relations with the broader Earth community. Religions link humans to the larger matrix of indeterminacy and mystery from which life arises, unfolds, and flourishes.

Religious cosmologies describe the experience of origination and change in relation to the natural world. Religious rituals and symbols arise out of cosmologies and are grounded in the dynamics of nature. They provide rich resources for encouraging spiritual and ethical transformation in human life. This is true for example in Buddhism, which sees change in nature and the cosmos as a potential source of suffering for the human. Confucianism and Daoism, on the other hand, affirm nature's changes as the source of the Dao. In addition, the death-rebirth cycle of nature serves as an inspiring mirror for human life, especially in the Western monotheistic traditions of Judaism, Christianity, and Islam. All religions translate natural cycles into rich tapestries of interpretive meanings that encourage humans to move beyond tragedy, suffering, and despair. Human struggles expressed in religious symbolism find their way into a culture's art, music, and literature. By linking human life and patterns of nature, religions have provided a meaningful orientation to life's continuity, as well as to human diminishment and death. In addition, religions have helped to celebrate the gifts of nature such as air, water, and food that sustain life.

Religions have been significant catalysts for humans in coping with change and transcending suffering, while at the same time grounding humans in nature's rhythms and Earth's abundance. Mankind needs beliefs that respect and honour spiritual responsibility, that speak to humanity, rising above religious, racial and ethnic differences. Beliefs that reveal the meaning and purpose of life, and hence the ethics needed for our survival.

Living a Spiritual Life is open to anyone at any time. It is a liberating, simple, joyous and deeply satisfying life. It provides perspective on troubling and disturbing events, while struggling to come to terms with, and overcome, difficulties, as a necessary part of life.

A Spiritual Life is equally respectful of yourself, others and the world around you. Your life, your needs and desires are no more and no less important than anyone else's.

You take and use what you really need, not everything you want. Spirituality demands that you accept responsibility for what is happening in the here and now. How you live your life now is the issue.

Your individual life is a privilege, a gift to be honoured, an opportunity to participate in the creation and promotion of greater harmony and stability in the material world of the life cycle.

Being spiritually responsible is built on simple things: planting a tree, helping a neighbour, being politically aware so that you carefully consider your vote, supporting a sharing of sustainable wealth with all mankind.

Taking responsibility gives real purpose to life, and how you do that provides real meaning.

Making the ethical choice in everything we do is practising a spiritual life. Not looking away, but doing everything we personally can to create a fairer, more respectful world: because a fairer world respects others and the planet as much as yourself. A fairer world creates a sustainable world, and a sustainable world enhances the stability and order of the spiritual life of the cosmos.

The spiritual and the worldly life are secretly mirrored by the psychic underworld, site or our fantasies, dreams and desires, passions and basic instincts.

Each of us contains a Dr. Jekyll and a Mr. Hyde, a more pleasant persona for everyday wear, and a hiding, night-time self that remains hushed up much of the time. Negative emotions and behaviours – rage, jealousy, shame, lying, resentment, lust, greed, suicidal and murderous tendencies – lie concealed just beneath the surface, masked by our more proper selves. It is the personal shadow, which remains untamed, unexplored territory to most of us.

The shadow is one of the major, inherited structures in the unconscious, known as archetypes. They contain preformed characteristics, personal qualities, and traits shared with all other human beings. They are living psychic forces within the human psyche.

The personal shadow develops naturally in every young child. As we identify with ideal personality characteristics such as politeness and generosity, which are reinforced in our environment, we shape the 'Good boy/girl' Self. At the same time, we bury in the shadow those qualities that don't fit our self image, such as rudeness and selfishness. The ego and the shadow develop in tandem, creating each other out of the same life experience.

We see the shadow mostly indirectly, in the distasteful traits and actions of other people, out there where it is safer to observe it. When we react to laziness or stupidity, sensuality, or spirituality, this may be our own shadow showing.

The shadow may erupt unexpectedly, but usually it recedes just as quickly, because meeting the shadow can be a frightening and shocking experience to our self-image.

It's common to meet the shadow at midlife, when one's deeper needs and values tend to change direction. This calls for breaking old habits and cultivating dormant talents. If we don't stop to heed the call, and continue to move in the same life direction, we will remain unaware of what midlife has to teach.

Meeting the shadow calls for slowing the pace of life, listening to the body's cues, and allowing ourselves time to be alone, in order to digest the cryptic messages from the hidden world.

We live in a time of critical excesses. For many people, the unacceptable qualities of excess go directly into the unconscious shadow, and these extremes take the form of symptoms: intensely negative feelings and actions, neurotic suffering, psychosomatic illnesses, depression, and substance abuse.

The shadow goes by many familiar names: the disowned self, the lower self, the dark twin or brother in bible and myth, the double, repressed self, alter ego, id. When we come face-to-face with our darker side, we use metaphors to describe these shadow encounters: meeting our demons, wrestling with the devil, descent to the underworld, dark night of the soul, midlife crisis. However, a right relationship with the shadow offers us a great gift: to lead us back to our buried potentials.

We all have a shadow. Or does our shadow have *us*?

Images Inside My Head

The psychologist Carl Jung 'revealed' the world of the unconscious and the creative energy structures of the archetypes. He addressed Christianity's central figure, Christ, as a symbol of the Self-image, the archetype of wholeness and completion.

Jesus became the collective figure whom the unconscious of his contemporaries expected to appear, and he took on those projections. Because of his lifestyle and deeds, Jesus exemplify the archetype of the Christ, or in Jung's psychological language, the Self, which is a more inclusive word for the inner image of god, which resides in every person.

The archetypal Christ is not limited to one man, Jesus, but can be seen as the potential "greater personality" in every individual. According to Jung, the life of Christ represents the various phases and expressions of the Self, as it undergoes incarnation in an individual ego. The various stages of the individuation process can be mirrored by living our individual lives as fully, as authentically, and as obediently (to a greater Source) as Jesus lived his.

'Taking up one's own cross', as Jesus invited his followers to do, and consciously realizing one's own particular pattern of wholeness, involves being suspended between successive pairs of opposites (like the physical crucifixion), with its corresponding suffering, and repeated death/rebirth experiences of the ego, as it learns to bow to the demands of the Self. However, consciously 'carrying one's life' in this way also provides the possibility of discovering the meaning of one's unique, individual life, and participating in life's larger purposes. It means the possibility of discovering one's vocation to make meaning out of the mystery of existence.

Many of the actions of Jesus provide a metaphor for personal transformation. Jesus takes water and transforms it into wine. That can be heard as a parable of how ordinary people (who are like water) can be taken by Jesus, and transformed into something analogous to excellent wine. Jesus does not just produce excellent wine from nowhere, though; he takes what is available, the ordinary water that they have to hand, and orders that the jars be filled to the brim, before he undertakes his work of transformation.

Similarly, in the story of the feeding of thousands of people with a few loaves, Jesus takes what is available, the handful of loaves that have been brought into the desert, and transforms them into superabundance, plenty for everyone and much left over. Heard as a parable about personal transformation, it seems that Jesus is saying that if we feel we have depleted resources, and do not have enough time and energy to cope, he has the ability to take what time and energy we have and transform it into plenty.

Upon following Jesus' instructions, the fishermen's catch was so great that their nets were about to break. The message is again clear. Without Jesus, the experience of life is one of depletion and lack of fulfilment; with Jesus there is a promise of super-abundance.

Long before Physicists, Psychologists or Christians had even conceived a hint of their theories, masters of thought and reflection were inspiring and supporting today's notions of paradox, entropy and uncertainty, painting their words in stone, wood and leather tablets, with original, magisterial strokes.

For those who stepped outside their comfort zone and changed, millennia ago in ancient and remote regions of the world: *we salute you!*

Do More and Accomplish Less

The Chinese, like the Indians, believed that there is an ultimate reality which underlies and unifies the multiple things and events we observe: 'complete', 'all-embracing', 'the whole', all refer to the 'One thing'. They called this reality the Tao, which originally meant 'the Way', term also employed by Jesus the Christ to define his teaching and work. It is the way, or process, of the universe, the order of nature. Tao is the cosmic process in which all things are involved; the world is seen as a continuous flow and change.

The Chinese believe that whenever a situation develops to its extreme, it is bound to turn around and become its opposite. This basic belief has given them courage and perseverance in times of distress, and has made them cautious and modest in times of success. 'The sage avoids excess, extravagance and indulgence'.

In the Chinese view, it is better to have too little than to have too much, and better to leave things undone than to overdo them, because although one may not get very far this way, one is certain to go in the right direction. Just as the man who wants to go further and further East will end up in the West, those who accumulate more and more money in order to increase their wealth will end up being poor. Modern industrial society is continuously trying to increase the 'standard of living', and thereby decreasing the quality of life for all its members.

Change does not occur as a consequence of some force, but rather as a tendency which is innate in all things and situations. The movements of the Tao are not forced upon it, but occur naturally and spontaneously. Acting in harmony with nature thus means for the Taoists acting spontaneously, and according to one's true nature. It means trusting one's intuitive intelligence, which is innate in the human mind, just as the laws of change are innate in all things around us.

The actions of the Taoist sage arise out of his intuitive wisdom. Such a way of acting is called *wu-wei* or non-action: refraining from activity contrary to nature, so one is in harmony with the Tao, makes one's actions successful. The Taoists believed that by displaying the feminine, mystic, yielding qualities of human nature, it is easiest to lead a perfectly balanced life in harmony with Tao.

In the last chapter of the book, I say thank you again, and good-bye; I'm putting all my eggs in this basket, and my neck on the line, by taking a quantum leap and introducing you to a whole new level of the game. But you deserve it.

May you reach your personal and spiritual peak in life, and stay there forever.

The Unity of All Things

The most important characteristic of the Eastern world view – one could almost say the essence of it – is the awareness of the unity and mutual interrelation of all things and events, the experience of all phenomena in the world as manifestations of a basic oneness. All things are seen as interdependent and inseparable parts of this cosmic whole; as different manifestations of the same ultimate reality.

The basic oneness of the universe is not only the central characteristic of the mystical experience, but is also one of the most important revelations of modern physics. It becomes apparent at the atomic level and manifests itself more and more as one penetrates deeper into matter, down into the realm of subatomic particles. The various models of subatomic physics express again and again, in different ways, the same insight – that the constituents of matter, and the basic phenomena involving them, are all interconnected, interrelated and interdependent; that they cannot be understood as isolated entities, but only as integrated parts of the whole.

At the atomic level, the solid material objects dissolve into patterns of probabilities; and not even probabilities of things, but rather *probabilities of interconnections*. Quantum theory forces us to see the universe not as a collection of physical objects, but rather as a complicated web of relations between the various parts of a unified whole.

The material object becomes something different from what we now see, not a separate object on the background, or in the environment of the rest of nature, but an indivisible part of the unity of all that we see. Things derive their being and nature by mutual dependence, and are nothing in themselves.

An elementary particle is not an independent entity. It is, in essence, a set of relationships that reach outward to other things.

The world is a perfect network of mutual relations where all things and events interact with each other in an infinitely complicated way. In Eastern mysticism, this universal interwovenness always includes the human observer and his or her consciousness, and this is also true in atomic physics.

The idea of 'participation instead of observation' has been formulated in modern physics only recently, but it is an idea which is well known to any student of mysticism. Observer and observed, subject and object, are not only inseparable but also become indistinguishable. The mystics in deep meditation arrive at a point where the distinction between observer and observed breaks down completely, where subject and object fuse into a unified undifferentiated whole.

In the psychic sub-atomic world of our personal Unconscious, there exist *pairs of opposites*, energies in oscillatory tension. The greater the tension between the pair of opposites, the greater will be the energy that comes from them, and the greater the energy, the stronger will be its attracting power. From a high level of oscillation within the Unconscious, a consolidated and lasting product can be 'manifested', whether an attitude, a lasting psychic process, or the blueprint for a process or an object in the material world .

The shadow archetype in the personal Unconscious, as well as the Self, are examples of pure oscillation. Following the Laws of Thermodynamics, when the level of oscillation decreases towards maximum entropy, unbalance and uncertainty also diminish, and the oscillating energy increases its consolidation towards matter. Through a transition from an improbable to a probable state, differences equalise, entropy increases, and shapes start taking form. The observer, the creating oscillation, changes into being one with the observed, the manifested process.

Thus, you may end up creating, converting into, and attracting, what you think. You interweave, intercept, cross paths, with that which is taking form before you. You coincide, meet, synchronise with, your goal, desired outcome, or vision, and this is how *you can get what you want*: by placing yourself in direct contact with, and being part of, your creation, aware of the unity and mutual interrelation of all things and events.

For those about to change: do live long and prosper, full of joy and achievement. We salute you!

Alfonso Vonscheidt

The Inspiralist

London, May 2012

www.ingramcontent.com/pod-product-compliance
Ingram Content Group UK Ltd.
Pitfield, Milton Keynes, MK11 3LW, UK
UKHW021051270726
13967UKWH00012B/575